BELLEVUE

ITS FIRST
100 YEARS

A typical farm in 1887 was that of Daniel Whitney and his wife Sarah Jane
Green. This picture, taken in 1887, includes their invaluable helper, a horse
named Charley. This was located near today's junction of Northup Way and
124th Ave. NE. Another cabin built a year later at the spot site has been moved
and is on display at Kelsey Creek Park. (See photograph on page 48.)

BELLEVUE

ITS FIRST
100 YEARS

Lucile McDonald

With a new introduction by Charles P. LeWarne

Bellevue Historical Society
Bellevue, Washington

First Printing 1984
Revised Edition 2000

Publisher's Cataloging-in-Publication

McDonald, Lucile Saunders, 1898–
     Bellevue, its first 100 years / Lucile McDonald ;
with a new introduction by Charles P. LeWarne.
     -- 2nd ed.
     p. cm.
     Bellevue, its first one hundred years
     Includes bibliographical references and index.
     ISBN: 0-9700800-0-X

     1. Bellevue (Wash.)--History. 2. Bellevue (Wash.)--
Social life and customs.   I. Title. II. Title:
Bellevue, its first one hundred years

     F899.B39M38 2000   979.7'77
                                   QBI00-722

Book coordination, design and production services provided by The History Bank, Woodinville, WA and Edmonton, AB.

Cover photo credits: Early Bellevue courtesy Museum of History and Industry; modern-day Bellevue courtesy Roger Hoesterey.

Printed in Canada

ABOUT THE 1984 EDITION

The Bellevue Friends of the Library published Lucile McDonald's "unique history of Bellevue," which began in the spring of 1983, when Lynn Lancaster, head librarian, suggested the idea to its Board of Trustees, Glorene Stevick, president.

Those who actually typed and proofread the manuscript included Blanche Carpenter, Ginger Fulton, Arlyn Kerr, Julie Kerr, Sharon Mayfield, Jackie Smelser, Milly Trueblood, Harriet Watters, Malia Watters, and Ken Watters. Susan Christie, Jackie Smelser, Arlyn Kerr and Harriet Watters collected and sorted photographs for the book. Ken Watters' also provided technical assistance organizing and transmitting the text to the printer and also donated his aircraft and pilot services for aerial photography. Harriet N. Watters and Susan H. Christie were co-presidents of the Bellevue Friends of the Library. Watters was book committee chair, Christie photograph committee chair.

ACKNOWLEDGMENTS

The Bellevue Historical Society would like to thank many individuals and public and private groups for their assistance in making this revised edition of Lucile McDonald's 1984 centennial history of Bellevue a reality.

Charles P. LeWarne provided the wonderful new introduction not only to this book, but to the author herself and of course to Bellevue as it has evolved since Ms. McDonald wrote about it.

The new 33-page introduction provides a wonderfully appropriate sprucing up of the story of Bellevue, repairing many politically incorrect or too-brief or unsubstantiated bits of oral history.

The original book, published by Bellevue Friends of the Library, was the first history of the city, and this revision remains essentially still the only comprehensive history of Bellevue. It was The Historical Society's intent to see that Ms. McDonald's book remained in print, even though it has been criticized in the past for its lack of solid, verified history and reliance on Ms. McDonald's talents for weaving a tale and listening to oldtimers from Bellevue.

Typographical, spelling, factual and other errors were corrected. Getting the book done, as well as ensuring the improved accuracy, was under the direct guidance of volunteer Libby Walgamott, without whom the project would never have seen the light of the day. Assisting Ms. Walgamott were a group of volunteers with a common passion, seeing this book—an improved book—available for everyone to read.

The editorial board for this project included Norman Blye, Phyllis Fenwick, Robert and Eloise Hennig, Dr. Lorraine McConaghy, Dick McDonald (Lucile's son), Pat Sandbo, Paul Vander Hoek, James Warren and Gini Wisner. Thanks also to Mary Ellen Piro whose knowledge and assistance was invaluable to the project.

Grant money for the book was received from:

King County
Landmarks & Heritage Commission
Hotel/Motel Tax Fund

Bellevue Friends of the Library, which not only donated money to the project, but also assigned their copyright for the 1984 book to The Bellevue Historical Society.

In-kind contributions were also provided by Norman Bolotin and The History Bank, Charles P. LeWarne and The Bellevue Historical Society.

INTRODUCTION
TO THE 2000 REVISION

Charles P. LeWarne

When Lucile McDonald moved to a small house in south Bellevue in 1972, she was, in her mid-seventies, doubtless the most prominent woman journalist-historian in the Northwest. Raised and educated in Oregon, she had pioneered in a man's field working for several newspapers with stints in Alaska, South America, and the Middle East. She had become best known in the Seattle area during recent decades writing for *The Seattle Times*, especially for her series of popular Sunday magazine articles on both well known and obscure topics and individuals in Northwest history. She had written all or part of thirty-five books, most of them historical, for children and adults. Indeed, her move to Bellevue was short in distance as she had lived previously a few miles north in Kirkland. She had turned her writing efforts to eastside papers and topics, and in 1977 began writing some 400 local history columns for the *Bellevue Journal-American*.

It was hardly surprising that McDonald would turn her attention to the history of that thriving eastside city or that the Bellevue Friends of the Library would agree to publish it. The result was *Bellevue: Its First 100 Years*, published in 1984. Ranging from the earliest period of white settlement to the date of publication, it has a distinct journalistic style; its homey, somewhat folksy narrative is laced with abundant names and anecdotes. This, indeed, is one of the book's strengths. McDonald was able to interview many persons who had lived as children and even adults in a much earlier Bellevue and thus recounted their recollections and impressions. Occasionally she utilized the academic tools and resources of the professional historian, most particularly in the final chapters. Yet as her biographer—a sympathetic historian—notes, she tells stories but rarely questions sources or provides analyses. McDonald was primarily a very good teller of stories.[1]

As she wrote she acknowledged the obvious: in the late 1970s and early 1980s Bellevue was changing significantly from the community she lived in and described to a more citified environment. "THE CHARACTER OF BELLEVUE CHANGES" is the title of one of her late brief sections. And of course she was correct. Bellevue was fanning out horizontally to the east and vertically with high-rise buildings. It was annexing areas, changing its downtown to clearly urban proportions, acquiring industries new to mankind, experiencing great growth in property values, and reinventing its infrastructure. "When the city in the fall of 1981 decided to rezone its downtown area and permit some skyscrapers to be built, its suburban days were over," she wrote. "A land rush and building boom resulted and Bellevue became the hottest real estate market on the West Coast." It is revealing that in the year 2000, a mere sixteen years after the book was published, McDonald's description of her own Bellevue seems distant and quaint.

These thoughts are the taking-off place for this essay to introduce a new printing of her valuable history. The present author, raised in Bellevue many years ago, has written elsewhere on the theme of "Bellevues I Have Known." In my view the history of Bellevue has a more than local significance; its growth has been emblematic of events occurring generally in American urban growth over the last century and more. I see Bellevue as having gone through four stages, each rather typical of trends occurring in a changing nation.

"There have been four distinctly different Bellevues," I wrote a few years back, "three of them telescoped into the six decades of my lifetime. Early residents knew Bellevue as a pioneer village, while I have experienced Bellevue the small town, Bellevue the burgeoning suburb, and now Bellevue the metropolitan 'edge city.' Beyond mere nostalgia, Bellevue's history reflects the broader scope of America's urban growth because each of the four Bellevues has coincided with and symbolized a trend characteristic of our maturing nation."[2] McDonald's book recounts the first three of those phases, and her final pages foresee the coming of the fourth.

———————————

The pioneering stage is the focus of approximately the first thirty pages of McDonald's book. Most Bellevue pioneers came from the growing town of Seattle across Lake Washington and were speculating that cheap land out from the city promised potential value. People had already moved north from the original village clustered around Yesler's mill and over the eastern slopes toward Lake Washington. Not surprisingly, a few also gazed across those waters to its opposite shore. William Meydenbauer, Aaron Mercer (least famous of the trio of brothers that included Thomas and Asa), Clark Sturtevant, and others acquired land claims along the water or just inland. Less known, but somewhat typical, were Angus and Elizabeth Mackintosh who acquired land around the small lake now called Lake Bellevue. The Civil War veteran "was active in [Seattle] real estate and investments," McDonald tells us. "He founded the Merchants National Bank, of which he was president, and apparently his interest in the Eastside was purely speculative. He suffered financial reverses in 1895 and died in 1904." The property was sold.

Such pioneers might visit their land-holdings, clear a spot of land, erect a cabin, and even reside briefly, but their activities were merely a phase of investments in Seattle's environs. McDonald relates some anecdotes about how these folk and their families fared on the Eastside. One early resident offered a delightful description of Mercer Slough as it was before the lowering of Lake Washington changed it forever. These individuals had some impact on Bellevue and the Eastside—their familiar names forever grace local sites—but their experiences there were transient.

McDonald moves on to describe, "Permanent Settlers," those persons and families who truly created the settlement that would become Bellevue. They would leave indelible imprints, and as McDonald tells their histories, the book becomes in a sense a series of short biographies. A permanent way of life got underway for these Bellevue pioneers. The village just above Meydenbauer Bay acquired a name, a system of trails and roads, schools, a church, a doctor and other institutions suggesting a real, settled community.

By the turn of the century, Bellevue was gaining occasional attention from area newspapers. She describes it as "barely noticeable dot on the landscape, its present business center devoted to a scattering of small rural homes, fenced garden plots, cows munching long grass, chickens cackling, horses plodding along lanes or roads that were mostly a pair of ruts. . . . [I]n 1896 an acre and a half tract with a small house was taxed only $3.27." Virgin timber land was changing to stump ranches and garden plots were planted. Men hunted near their homes. "The residents drew their water from wells, and kerosene lamps lighted their way to bed." McDonald shows an 1895 U.S. Geological Survey map that points out major geographical features.

According to McDonald, these pioneers had few encounters with Native Americans. "It was not Indian country," she wrote, merely noting canoes passing by, a theft from the Meydenbauer cabin, and a few long houses. Indeed, the Bellevue area was sparsely inhabited by the Duwamish people who lived primarily on the southern reaches of Lake Washington and its river tributaries, but they gave names to several significant landmarks around Bellevue.[3] The lives of the "lake people" who inhabited the shores of Lake Washington, Lake Sammamish, and smaller bodies differed somewhat from groups dependent on the salt waters or along rivers. The lakes provided kokanee, a landlocked version of the sockeye salmon, and other fish for their diets. Waterfowl were plentiful. Pelts of small animals such as muskrats, beaver, otter were useful, and wapato roots, water lilies, and cattails provided food as well as fibers for mats and baskets. The people developed nets and tools. A village called Sa'tsaka L was located alongside Mercer Slough near today's Factoria, and possibly a long house at Yarrow Bay housed a couple dozen people. There may have been a burial site on the north shore of Meydenbauer Bay. At the Treaty of Point Elliott in 1855, the Duwamish were forced to cede their lands, but the treaties of that time created rather than ended tension throughout much of Washington Territory.

The most serious confrontations between whites and Native Americans occurred in eastern Washington, but Indians threatened Seattle in January 1856. After crossing the Cascades, perhaps a hundred warriors followed a trail from the southern end of Lake Sammamish to rendezvous at Sa'tsaka L. They then canoed to present-day Leschi Park to launch their attack on Seattle. Quickly defeated, the Indians returned to Sa'tsaka L, destroying what they could along the way. Internal rivalry among several Indian groups led to further warfare in eastern King County. The next spring, a small army force canoed to the site of Newport Shores. The "numerous hearths, scattered ox bones, and abandoned stores of wheat and peas" convinced their leader "that 400 Indians had camped there on and off over the last few months, living off their plunder after their attack on Seattle. The war camp and three large long houses found further up a trail had been abandoned only recently." American troops pursued the Indian forces, and historian David Buerge contends that "the war that scarred the Eastside also hastened its settlement. Many volunteers marching through it were impressed by its fertility, especially the prairies of the Snoqualmie valley." They built a few stockades which later settlers used as homes and barns.[4] In fact, settlement in that area preceded that around Bellevue.

Early in the new century, Bellevue slid into a new phase. As the pioneering years ended, Bellevue became a prototypical small town during an era when such communities seemed to characterize national life. Small-town images have endured from colonial villages to the contemporary resurgence of interest in sparsely populated, essentially rural places. The popular culture has given us Norman Rockwell paintings, Sinclair Lewis novels, Andy Hardy movies, and, in our own times, Bart Simpson's Springfield. Notwithstanding differences regionally and over time, certain similarities appear: a gridiron design that often centered about a common square or park, a "Main Street" lined with stores and shops, a sense of solidarity and familiarity among citizens, economic efforts that provide some self-sufficiency and local marketing potential, clusters of governmental and social institutions, homespun entertainment including programs, athletics, and civic celebrations, and ultimately a decline or change as circumstances change. In 1900, Washington, like many states, was dominated by rural areas and small towns. Six of every ten persons lived in areas defined as rural. Seventy-two of the 85 incorporated towns had populations of less than 2,500 and 54 less than 1,000; Bellevue was among the countless other villages and crossroads that were not incorporated.[5]

McDonald devotes about 137 pages to Bellevue's small-town era. A few stores and shops began to appear along a road soon called "Main Street." Most of the town was laid out in the traditional gridiron, and permanent social institutions, groups and clubs began to thrive. A sense of identity and community developed as the number of residents slowly increased. To the east, individual farms and isolated houses were interspersed amidst woodlands on rolling hills.

When McDonald wrote, many Bellevue residents of the small-town era—some from the earliest phase—still lived there and they shared their recollections.

Early on, there was no certainty that Main Street would become the heart of this community. Outlying settlements had their own characteristics. Midlakes developed near Lake Sturtevant as the local commercial center when a feed store and then other businesses were built along a north-south spur of the Northern Pacific Railroad. Trains lessened dependence on irregular boat traffic across Lake Washington. South of Midlakes, the Hewitt-Lea lumber mill at Wilburton made that, in McDonald's view, the industrial center. Farther east, settlers in the Highland area united to form a chapter of the National Grange. Early in the century a group of artists founded Beaux Arts Colony along Lake Washington, and farther south efforts to encourage heavy industry led to a community aptly named Factoria.

Within a few years, however, the small-town atmosphere of Bellevue would concentrate on the village at the head of Meydenbauer Bay. The first business was the grocery and general store of Patrick McGauvran who arrived in 1908. A simple frame structure, it was remembered as "a genuine old-fashioned place with open barrels of peanut butter and crackers and all other things that were needed in this remote area. The Masonic lodge was upstairs."

The sense of community identity was growing. Groups organized to promote the town and to develop social activities and athletic events. During the 1920s the Bellevue Businessmen's Association and the Bellevue Community Club were formed as was the Women's Club. And Bellevue began the community celebration that was to make it known and draw throngs of visitors each June, the Strawberry Festival. Serving locally grown berries, it grew from a small school yard gathering in 1925 to an annual event of regional renown. In 1935, 15,000 people were said to have attended.

For most, small-town Bellevue was a comfortable if not spectacular town. Two world wars and the Great Depression touched lives, but the author holds nostalgic childhood memories of a Norman Rockwell kind of place: "Our community had its share of social divisions, quarrels, jealousies and a tiny collection of busybodies and characters. Yet we who lived in small-town Bellevue knew who we were and what we were and that we belonged. Life carried a sense of identity along with security and certainty. . . . The mythology of small-town America usually brings to mind villages in New England or the Midwest. In the far Northwest, Bellevue was as representative of small-town America as a community could be."[6]

Yet the true picture was not so idyllic for all. Sometimes meshing with but not truly within the visible community, some three hundred persons of Japanese ancestry, a few with roots to the turn of the century, raised vegetables and berries on parcels scattered out from town.

Bellevue's small-town isolation began to evaporate as World War II and other events combined to alter it and other communities. The proximity of a city with 300,000 persons just across Lake Washington and the common use of automobiles foreshadowed change. For years Eastsiders had taken boats or had driven cars to Seattle for work, schooling, shopping, recreation and other visits. Early visionaries had proposed a bridge across the lake to the metropolis. During the 1930s Bellevue residents, including wealthy Seattle publisher Miller Freeman and local newspaper editor Al Whitney began to actively promote the idea. The opening of the Lacey V. Murrow floating bridge—now part of Interstate 90—in the summer of 1940, however, did not bring immediate change because war intervened. But during the late forties, that bridge combined with the mushrooming population of the Northwest and apparent prosperity to virtually ensure a wave of movement out of Seattle into eastside suburbs. By 1950 Bellevue was clearly entering its next phase. It was becoming a Seattle suburb.

———————

American suburbs of the post-war years have been praised, pilloried, and parodied. Suburbia seemed to fulfill the American dream: " a single family home with a two-car garage, a barbecue pit and a basketball hoop surrounded by gardens" with easy access to the advantages of a large nearby city.[7] The sublime life of the working father, stay-at-home mom and 2.5 happy children enjoying a wholesome suburban life in the fifties became a staple of the new medium of television. But popular sociologists berated the "organization men" in grey flannel suits who lived there, and Pete Seeger ridiculed "little boxes made out of ticky-tacky."

Most of the final forty pages of McDonald's narrative describe Bellevue the suburb of Seattle. She lived in this community and knew it firsthand; yet, the narrative includes few of the folksy, charming reminiscences and anecdotes that graced earlier pages. The book becomes primarily an account of growth and change, new stores, new developments, new associations, and major players. We learn about the beginnings of the Bellevue Shopping Square, the Pacific Northwest Arts and Crafts Fair, ubiquitous housing developments and instant neighborhoods, a revised infrastructure and physical changes, but there is little feel for what it was like to live there, for the excitement of growth and change. For that we must turn elsewhere.

The movement of residents out of large cities to closeby environs is a constant factor in American life. Most often the trend involved a natural progression of residents to immediate outlying areas often aided by planners and developers, and sometimes following web-like patterns along well-trod paths, streetcar lines, and then auto highways. Thus Seattle had spread north and south and east to its lake shore; early in the twentieth century it enveloped existing communities into its city limits. The eastward movement, however, was blocked by the deep waters of Lake Washington, which stretched the entire length of the city. To be sure, highways curved north and south around the lake, and auto ferries sailed first from Bellevue, and then from Medina and Kirkland. Passenger-only boats crossed the lake. The growing small towns on the Eastside were within the orbit of the large city and more than a few Eastsiders managed the daily commute. But until the construction of two bridges—one replacing an existing, narrow structure from Enatai to Mercer Island and the other a ribbon of concrete continuing to Seattle—the lake remained a barrier to substantial suburban growth on the Eastside.

In the long run, the pressure from Eastsiders was enhanced by leaders from Seattle and eastern Washington (including Governor Clarence D. Martin of Cheney) who wanted a cross-state highway to feed directly into the state's largest city. But the struggle to build a bridge with unique floating pontoons is less a part of our story than how its existence affected Bellevue after the bridge was completed. When World War II ended, Bellevue and its eastside neighbors were primed for a wave of expansion scarcely imaginable a decade earlier. It would emerge from its small-town existence to become a quintessential American suburb.

Those changes were part of a national trend toward suburban expansion, but certain aspects were unique to Seattle which emerged from World War II a far different city than before. Following some immediate postwar dislocations and economic uncertainties, the city became larger and more cosmopolitan. Boeing emerged as the dominant mainstay of the economy, with a wartime plant ten miles south of Bellevue at Renton as well as the older, greatly expanded factories in Seattle. The growth of Boeing brought an influx of workers to the area, including highly trained and well paid engineers, and many were attracted to the suburbs. Veterans who had lived in or passed through the Northwest while serving in the military found it a desirable place to locate, and they were aided by the GI Bill and veterans' housing benefits. Seattle's population grew increasingly diverse as large numbers of African-Americans drawn to wartime opportunities remained. Asian-Americans continued to live in the area, including some of Japanese descent who slowly returned to former homes after wartime incarceration. Emerging suburbs often had a reputation for good schools and excellent cultural and recreational opportunities. All of these circumstances in the larger area played into the developments that would soon alter Bellevue.

Early effects of the changes were obvious. As bridge traffic replaced ferry runs, the new Overlake Transit Service provided bus service. At an intersection eight blocks north of Main Street, two new shopping structures had emerged. Lakeside Center was built by longtime resident and visionary James Ditty; on an opposite corner, Kay Neumann had opened a lumber and hardware store. But the shift of business activity north from the old town center was dramatized when the Bellevue Shopping Square opened in 1946 on several acres of old farm and orchard land.

The key figure was Kemper Freeman, destined to dominate the growth of Bellevue for the next 35 years. With his family's estate on Meydenbauer Bay, Freeman knew Bellevue well. He entered the family publishing business and other enterprises before he became excited by the potential of the Eastside and determined to build a well-designed, complete shopping center. Originally considering a location near Main Street, he shifted his sights several blocks north and proceeded to create the Bellevue Shopping Square.[8]

The Square, which McDonald describes well, portended a new kind of shopping complex designed for automobile traffic rather than pedestrians. Five hundred parking stalls ringed the first branch of Seattle's premier department store, Frederick & Nelson, and the perimeter was lined with shops. A "Food Center" resembled the old-time grocery less than a large department store specializing in foods. "The Square," proclaimed *The Bellevue American*, "is dedicated to the belief that people living in suburbs and country are entitled to the same conveniences of cities without the inconveniences of cities."[9]

The pressure of home seekers desiring to live on the Eastside required new housing neighborhoods. Vuecrest, built on the hillside homesteaded in the late 1800s by Patrick Downey and recently farmed by

Japanese and white Americans, offered expansive views which combined with elements of convenience and luxury to create a new kind of neighborhood. Architect-designed homes blended several features and building materials, and gardens were carefully landscaped. Similar developments would soon become commonplace, but in the late 1940s the concept of a pre-planned and refined neighborhood was new.[10]

Other subdivisions appeared amongst established neighborhoods. "The local names suggest country estate living—Evergreen Point, Killarney, Eastgate, Midlakes, Enatai, Tall Firs, Sherwood Forest," wrote a promotional brochure.[11] Some attracted specific groups of people: horse devotees at Bridle Trails Park, boat owners at Newport Shores,[12] and University professors at a cooperative community called Hilltop.[13] World War II veterans pooled resources to establish Norwood Village, a cooperative collection of small homes on a south Bellevue hillside. In such subdivisions newcomers were customarily strangers suddenly drawn together to establish a new community.

By the late 1940s and early 1950s, large residential developments were emerging east of the original Bellevue core. Just south of the Sunset Highway, the four lane cross-state connection to the floating bridge that became part of Interstate 90, George Bell and Ted Valdez put together the planned neighborhood of Eastgate with its own small shopping complex. Its success led to an even larger community to the north that would be known as Lake Hills. Bell and Valdez became the Eastside's major builders of moderately priced homes.

Lake Hills emerged as the largest planned development in the state. It sprawled over 1,200 acres of wetlands, fertile slopes and second growth timbered hills, some of it overlooking Lake Sammamish.[14] In 1955 R. H. "Dick" Conner acquired the property and prepared to create an instant community with streets, infrastructure, shopping and public areas, and houses, 4,000 of them. With John Anderson as the leading architect and

Bell and Valdez the principal builders, Lake Hills homes were a bit larger, better designed, and more nicely sited than most Eastgate houses, though less striking than many in established Bellevue. Amidst advertising hoopla, young couples stood in mud-filled plots surrounded by earthmoving equipment as they heard sales pitches and visualized their dream houses. The grand opening was grand indeed, and families began to settle in. Here as elsewhere, neighbors were strangers suddenly drawn to share their lives together and create a completely new community. There were amenities. The Lake Hills Community Club became a de facto government—soon warring with the developer over multiple unit housing—and a swim club was the center of social life. Perhaps 75 percent of the men were Boeing workers.[15] After years of near independence, in 1969 the people of Lake Hills determined that their interests would be best served by joining Bellevue and, on the third try, voted for annexation.

Rapid growth brought disruptions throughout the Bellevue area. Dozens or hundreds of pieces of heavy machinery dug and droned throughout the community. New roads were built and old ones widened, straightened, and paved. Power lines and water pipes and sewers were going in all over town. The Overlake School District, a wartime merger of several small entities, became the Bellevue School District and hurriedly put up new buildings and expanded its staff to meet the demands of young families. Shopping malls were sprinkled about the area, highlighted by Crossroads several miles east of traditional Bellevue.

The newcomers brought a more sophisticated set of activities than the erstwhile small town. The Strawberry Festival was a wartime casualty, but the Pacific Northwest Arts and Crafts Fair, centered at the Square became a mainstay of the new culture. A defunct golf club near Medina was resuscitated and new ones built east and north of town. A little theater and a riding club were formed, and a yacht club acquired the old Wildwood Park. Suburban Bellevue was vastly different from the small town of only a decade or so earlier, but praise was not universal. The old townsfolk and the new (some of whom were more focused toward Seattle than Bellevue) did not always see eye to eye. Occasional newspaper articles ridiculed the "plastic" community, and the increasingly well heeled town became the butt of jokes by radio personalities. A feature article in *Seattle Magazine* that purported to sum up the virtues and problems of suburban life touched a sensitive nerve. "[T]here is one place hereabouts which, more than any other, proudly proclaims its own unique, nonmetropolitan identity," the author commented, "and that place, of course, is the city (or the area, or the mentality) that is called Bellevue."[16]

For several years Bellevue claimed to be the fastest growing community in Washington, and one of the fastest growing in the nation. When it incorporated in 1953, 5,940 residents lived on about five square miles close to Meydenbauer Bay, but the small-town atmosphere was disappearing. Over the next several decades, the population and the town exploded, moving eastward and almost annually annexing both small and large areas to the city. By the middle seventies Bellevue reached seven miles from Lake Washington to Lake Sammamish.

As Lucile McDonald wrote her history of Bellevue early in the 1980s, the transformation to a true city was becoming apparent. Following descriptions of the changing character of the town, her final section is called "Rising Skyline." The former pioneer village, small town, and suburb was becoming a city.

———————

In 1991, *Washington Post* columnist Joel Garreau keynoted a conference on the "Emerging City" at Bellevue's plush new Hyatt-Regency Hotel at Bellevue Place. Its twin towers were located kitty-corner across a bustling intersection from where the Bellevue Square had buried fields and orchard less than five decades earlier.

A specialist on urban issues, Garreau had recently published a book entitled *Edge City*.[17] His thesis was as clear as the view from the top of the Hyatt-Regency: "edge cities" had grown up adjacent to older, established cities that they had come to rival and even overshadow. These new metropolitan entities had all the features of their older neighbors plus other characteristics.

Garreau's edge cities had four essential characteristics. They had to:

- contain at least five million square feet of office space and 600,000 square feet of retail space;

- have a workday population that marks the location as primarily a work center rather than a residential suburb;

- be perceived locally as an end destination for a wide mix of daily activities including work, shopping and entertainment; and

- have been essentially residential or rural thirty years earlier.[18]

Garreau listed 123 edge cities that existed in the United States in 1991. The only one in Washington was Bellevue.[19]

A striking component of Bellevue's change was the dramatic population increase composed of persons moving in and by the annexation of additional, usually newly settled, areas. By 1960 Bellevue's population had reached 12,800, more than double the incorporation estimate of fewer than 6,000 inhabitants just seven years earlier. The population then increased five times to 62,000 in 1970; to 74,000 in 1980; 87,000 in 1990; and 106,200 (an official state estimate) in 1999. By 1970 it was the fourth largest city in the state, following Seattle, Spokane, and Tacoma. (Annexations and growth pushed Vancouver to fourth place in 1999 with Bellevue fifth.)[20]

The physical changes in the city and its boundaries were striking. No longer was Bellevue a shoreline village. Its boundaries crept east and occasionally southward over rolling hills, fields, and woodlands that were increasingly speckled with housing developments and small shopping centers. Many annexations included only the few acres of a property owner or two. But some were spectacularly large. The annexations of Woodridge and Sherwood Forest in 1964 brought in 1,600 acres, and five years later Lake Hills and Sammamish additions 2,500 more.[21] During the 1990s almost four square miles were brought in, mostly south of Interstate 90, and Bellevue covered almost thirty-one square miles. There was little more potential area left to annex. Bellevue stretched seven miles from the shores of Lake Washington to Lake Sammamish and—with irregular borders—almost ten miles from north to south.

Nor do such figures tell the whole story. Bellevue had emerged as the center of the Eastside. Typically suburban just a few years earlier, Bellevue became the hub of its own circle of suburbs, most of them incorporated and many of them affluent: Medina, Evergreen Point, Hunts Point, Yarrow Point, Clyde Hill, and Newcastle. Some borders with older neighbors such as Kirkland, Redmond, Issaquah, and Renton were indistinguishable, and these cities often moved about the orbit of Bellevue. By the 1990s the Eastside was a megalopolis.

The physical changes also extended upward. In her final pages, McDonald described a skyline that "had begun sprouting in the 1970s [and] was changing each month with the erection of tall structures. The Skyline Tower is 24 stories high, One Bellevue Center 22 stories and Plaza Center 16 stories." Other high rises were being planned. Only two decades earlier, the trend had begun when Puget Sound Power and Light erected its headquarters, a meager four stories. McDonald possibly anticipated the continuing climb of distinctive high rise structures that would dominate the skyline, their heights accentuated by their presence on the hillside alongside downtown. Bellevue's bevy of glass-enclosed towers, several rising over 25 stories—one in unique copper tones—began to emulate Seattle. As the 21st century began, construction of a 36-story tower, Bellevue's tallest, was getting underway just east of the Square.[22] Indeed, ubiquitous construction cranes were as much a part of the skyline as the structures they built.

Downtown itself was spreading north and east. In the early 1980s, Kemper Freeman enlarged and enclosed the Bellevue Square and brought in a multitude of new stores and restaurants. The fashionable shopping complex became a prototype for others. Main Street, once the heart of small-town Bellevue, still had only two lanes but its shops became increasingly upscale; in 2000 it is becoming edged with multi-story office buildings and condominiums. As vacant spots filled with stores, mini-malls and offices, Bellevue's downtown crept east over the hillside and across Interstate 405, eventually embracing the pioneering commercial center of Midlakes.

Growth was not confined to downtown Bellevue. In 1964 the Crossroads Shopping Center opened to serve residents well east of town. It had the accouterments of the larger Square including a major department store, shops and eating places, ample parking space, even an ice skating rink and a little theater.

Meanwhile, a group of developers promoted the concept that "the *geographic centroid* of the entire Eastside" was amongst undeveloped wood and pasture land midway between Lake Washington and Lake Sammamish. They started to plan Overlake Park, a potential rival to downtown Bellevue. Over time, the initial plans changed, but a combination commercial and retail complex emerged that crossed the Bellevue-Redmond city lines. With clean new high tech industries such as United Controls and retail stores such as Sears as the nucleus, numerous other businesses followed. In time, the huge Microsoft campus located there.[23] South of old Bellevue, shopping centers at Eastgate and Factoria were the first of several developments that straddled Interstate 90.

Major businesses and industries had come to Bellevue slowly, with the headquarters of Puget Sound Power and Light (now Puget Sound Energy) downtown and then a major Safeway distribution center near Midlakes. The Bellefield Office Park was a nicely styled complex amidst marshy ponds that had once been part of Mercer Slough. Employers increasingly chose Bellevue as a site for their businesses. At the end of the 20th century, *The Seattle Times* called the Eastside the "region's most dynamic business center." Eight of the 141 top Pacific Northwest companies had headquarters in Bellevue, with many more in neighboring towns. Most were high tech industries but Bellevue was also the home of such longtime giants as Puget Sound Energy, PACCAR, and First Mutual Savings Bank.[24] A City study concluded that Bellevue had 121,000 jobs, eleven percent of the total in all King County, and expected the increasing job market to continue.[25]

Of all the new eastside industries, the growth of the Microsoft Corporation was the most dramatic. After humble origins and its beginnings in Albuquerque, founder Bill Gates returned to his Seattle roots in 1978 and located the fledgling company in a bank building in downtown Bellevue. Within two years its rapid rise necessitated a move and Microsoft opened a constantly expanding complex on Northup Way, between Bellevue and Kirkland. The eventual move to the large sprawling campus above Lake Sammamish took the company just across city lines to Redmond, but its effect on Bellevue and all the Eastside was immense. Satellite and related computer technology companies have developed around the giant in many locations, creating a technology core to rival California's Silicon Valley.

By the middle 1980s traffic across Lake Washington from Seattle to the Eastside was greater than that westbound into the city. Bellevue and its neighbors were no longer just "bedroom communities." Moreover, traffic amongst eastside communities was increasing, with Bellevue at the hub. It became almost unnecessary for persons to go to Seattle for work or to shop for either mundane goods or highly priced and unique items. Most everything seemed to be available in Bellevue.

Cultural and recreational aspects were enhanced. Events from earlier days continued and broadened: the Arts and Crafts Fair, the Bellevue Philharmonic Orchestra, and the Bellevue Art Museum. Clusters of hotels and fine restaurants appeared, most notably along Interstate 405. The nearby Meydenbauer Center became a site for small conferences and other offerings, shows, and performances, and new such centers were being proposed. The local branch of the King County Library moved into a large building which won architectural awards. The early, weekly *Bellevue American* went through changes and mergers to become a daily newspaper. Bellevue Community College, nestled in woods just off Interstate 90 became one of the largest community colleges in the Northwest offering diverse programs. Overlake Memorial Hospital, which had begun as a major effort by community volunteers in the suburban years, became a regional leader. The former high school site was developed into Downtown Park, and other parks were designed including one at Kelsey Creek where pioneer children had fished. A walking and biking trail wound between Lakes Washington and Sammamish. One of the West's most elegant and scenic golf courses appeared on a hilltop south of Bellevue.

But growth brought questions common to many urban places. Where was Bellevue going and how successfully could it handle rapid expansion? Even in the 1930s James Ditty had visualized a city of well over 100,000 people, an outrageous thought at the time. The construction of the first Lake Washington bridge and then the second, with Bellevue well located about midway between them, seemed to assure the town would experience great changes. When Bellevue incorporated in 1953, its far-sighted planning director, Fred Herman, set the stage for handling extensive growth, and those efforts led *Look Magazine* to select Bellevue as an "All-

American City." Often growth seemed to outdistance the best of planning, but in the 1990s the state's Growth Management Act required cities to plan for future growth and determine where it could and would occur.

Such efforts were sometimes met with skepticism and prompted civic discussions about growth and how much it should be regulated. Some persons feared that rapid expansion and sprawl could cause a city to lose a sense of its own identity and a true feeling of community. And it seemed that a city clearly designed to accommodate automobile transportation neglected its pedestrians. It is a situation that is changing. Main Street still retains a semblance of a conventional small town. The Bellevue Square itself suggests a small-town atmosphere but within an expansive, covered environment, and a late 1990s development called the "Bellevue Galleria" hopes to create a "people place." After many years of neglect and decline, the Crossroads Shopping Center was redesigned to become a more inviting place with entertainment, games, and amenities to attract families and varied groups, "the social hub of one of Bellevue's most populous and ethnically diverse neighborhoods."[26]

All about Bellevue were signs of affluence, in the upscale boutiques and downtown stores, in the dress of the shoppers, and in the automobiles that brought them there. The 1995 average household income in the Bellevue area, some of it outside the city limits was $78,800, nearly 30% higher than in King County as a whole. That income had been rising more than five percent annually in recent years.[27] Homes that might have been labeled mansions a few years earlier no longer seemed unusual. Fine new developments spread across fields and wound over hills, many of them now south of Interstate 90. Some of the newly wealthy could afford to purchase houses for several hundred thousand dollars and demolish them to build something larger and grander.

But wealth was not the entire story, and economic disparities that often mark urban areas were also present in the new Bellevue. Ever since the growth spurts of the fifties, Bellevue leaders had been trying to shed its image as an enclave of wealth. As Bellevue became increasingly urban, pockets of poverty became evident, often but not exclusively in the Crossroads area. Many of the poor included racial minority newcomers, a rising population of elderly persons, and workers on substandard incomes. Living costs were becoming such that many people who serviced Bellevue could not afford to live there. A *Seattle Post-Intelligencer* article subtitled "Poverty Rocks the Cradle" described the poor and noted that Bellevue had opened a "mini-city hall" at the Crossroads to handle the needs of people living nearby.[28] Two elementary schools in East Bellevue qualified for special federal funds because fifty percent of the students were eligible for free- or reduced-price lunches.[29]

The rising number of minority residents was another clue that Bellevue had become an urban place. Bellevue has been and is a predominantly white or Euro-American community. As in much of the Northwest, most people were descended from northern and western Europe including the British Isles. Yet, the minority population grew. Minority enrollment in the Bellevue School District increased from slightly over 16 percent in 1987 to more then 30 percent in 1997; Asians are the most consistently increasing group with Hispanic Americans also on the rise. Nine percent of all students in 1997 were enrolled in English-as-a-Second-Language classes, indicating that another language prevails at home. Bellevue school children speak more than fifty languages.[30]

The most recent federal census available—taken in April 1990—placed Bellevue's white population at 86.5%, with Asians and Pacific Islanders making up the far largest minority group (ten percent), followed by blacks at two percent. The number of Native Americans and other races was negligible. Interestingly, these ratios are slightly different than those for the state as a whole, which was 88.5% white in 1990 with only 4.3% of the population Asian. Bellevue, in other words, has a larger percentage of Asian residents than the rest of the state.[31] There are increasing numbers of Hispanics and immigrants from former Soviet Union countries.

Amongst language and cultural barriers in an unfamiliar society, there are notable success stories. One Vietnamese immigrant is sketched in Bellevue's 1999 self-study. A pilot in the South Vietnamese army, he came to the United States for training as a young man, learned English, and dreamed of returning. After the Vietnamese war ended, he spent seven years in a prison camp. In the early 1990s he brought his wife and baby to Bellevue. Having some knowledge of English, he trained at a vocational school to fix large appliances, excelling as a student. Presently he has a steady job at Sears but plans to open his own business. His wife, who learned English along the way, is studying business at the University of Washington. "The two are striving to improve their family's life and hope other family members currently living in Vietnam may be able to move to the US [sic]."[32] If not typical, perhaps their story is at least representative of the growing and improving role of newcomers in Bellevue and similar cities.

Bellevue boasts of a low crime rate, but a perception of crime exists. The Crossroads area has been a particular source of concern, as have some of the areas along Interstate 90. And several spectacular crimes received wide media coverage. A 1997 survey suggested that most people feel safe in their own neighborhoods but suspect that crime rates overall are increasing, an impression civic leaders deny.[33]

Perhaps the most universally recognized problem involves transportation. When eastside leaders were queried as to their concerns, this was evident: "Traffic stinks!" "People are crankier in the rear view mirror, they're on you." "Traffic has doubled since I've been here (eight years)." Bellevue was largely built for and impacted by automobiles. Two interstate highways intersect the city, and a major east-west state highway cuts through. The network of roads was built as the city expanded.[34]

As a city study noted, Bellevue had "developed as a typical suburb with housing, jobs and shopping located in separate areas. . . . In 1980, people drove to work, to pick up a quart of milk, and to meet most of their daily needs because they had no choice." With most people working in Seattle or at Boeing, the highway and transit systems had been designed to move them there. But employment opportunities grew on the Eastside, reducing the dominance of Seattle and Boeing. As Greater Seattle developed into one of the nation's worst areas for traffic congestion, Bellevue shared. Many residents view solving transportation problems as the greatest issue the city and region must face as they meet the 21st century.[35]

Transportation and other matters were regional as well as local issues. An earlier generation of Bellevue and Seattle leaders, some of them eastside residents, cooperated in a successful regional effort to clean up a polluted Lake Washington. That effort had been nationally heralded. How new issues would be solved and the extent of Bellevue's cooperation with regional entities would be questions to address in the 21st century.

In 1997, 402 randomly selected Bellevue residents were asked what they valued about Bellevue and what their hopes were for its future. Almost all of them liked their city and had moved there for its location. They felt good about the future because of the healthy economy, the potential for growth, leaders who shared their concern, a sense of quiet and of safety, and friendly neighbors. They were concerned about too much growth, traffic congestion, and crime.[36] One can only speculate how the residents of pioneer Bellevue, small-town Bellevue, or even suburban Bellevue, might have responded in their own times.

Recent demographic figures remind one that although Bellevue's population is and was largely white, there have been underlying strands of diverse cultures as well. Many citizens, Lucile McDonald among them, have underplayed this part of the city's past. Among the minority population, that of Japanese immigrants and Japanese-Americans who have lived in Bellevue from very early days is the most enduring. Many men came to Washington in the late 1800s to work on railroads, in mills, and at farming, and in time a substantial number settled in Seattle and raised families. In the Nihonmachi district, up the hill around Jackson Street and Yesler Way, they opened businesses catering to their own needs and the larger community.[37] McDonald gives a brief account of the Japanese of Bellevue, but recent interest and research enables a more full account.[38]

Many Japanese were farming on the Eastside in the first decade of the twentieth century when the total population was small and sparsely settled. Often working on recently logged land, they grubbed out stumps and underbrush and planted crops as best they could. Many men hoped to earn enough money to return to Japan, but instead became a part of the life around Bellevue. Because legislation denied them citizenship and limited land ownership, they often leased land or made informal arrangements with the property owner. Gradually the immigrants (Issei) and their American born children (Nisei, U.S. citizens) increased, and their truck farms and greenhouses were interspersed about much of present-day Bellevue from Yarrow Point east toward the Highland area and south to Factoria. They raised flower bulbs, peas, beans, lettuce, and other crops for the local and Seattle market. By the 1930s, their abundant crops of strawberries were celebrated throughout the region and shipped elsewhere: Japanese-American growers provided most of the berries served at the Strawberry Festival. Tom Matsuoka, who moved to Bellevue in the middle 1920s, helped organize and became business manager of the Bellevue Vegetable Growers Warehouse, a cooperative marketing arrangement with a building alongside the railroad tracks at Midlakes.

Despite apparent successes, persons of Japanese ancestry were not truly integrated into the larger Bellevue community. They formed their own associations, highlighted by the Bellevue Japanese American Citizens League, along with baseball and basketball teams for their young men and women. Their community club located just north of the present-day Bellevue Square was the center of many activities; children were schooled in the Japanese language and culture. The young were often caught up in a chasm between the traditional culture of their parents and the new American way of life which they were growing up in. Yet they rarely felt or were viewed as an integral part of the community. Laws that restricted land holding caused some to move elsewhere even before World War II.

On December 7, 1941, just hours after Japanese warplanes bombed Pearl Harbor, bringing the two nations into war, federal authorities started rounding up Japanese-American community leaders along the Pacific Coast despite little evidence of wrong doing. Matsuoka was taken into custody along with Asaichi Tsushima who had founded the language school, and Terumatsu Yabuki, a Yarrow Point greenhouse operator recently elected secretary of the Bellevue Japanese Community Association. False rumors about possible sabotage reached hysterical and unwarranted levels including stories of fields planted in arrows or lines of wire in berry fields directing Japanese planes to strategic targets. Military and political leaders, including prominent Eastsiders, urged that all persons of Japanese descent be incarcerated.

In mid-February 1942, President Franklin D. Roosevelt signed Executive Order 9066 which authorized the removal of all persons of Japanese descent, American citizens included, from along the Pacific Coast. This included about 13,000 from Washington. By now they fully realized that not just a few but all of them would be forced from homes and farms. While waiting, they planted and cared for their crops, even as spring harvest-time approached. Bellevue's Japanese were among the last to be called, but when the official notice came, they had only five days to get ready. They could take only the belongings they could carry. They sold property and furnishings at low cost, although some found friends who promised to look after things for them. On May 20, some sixty families from Bellevue, including over 300 men, women, and children, boarded trains at Kirkland, not knowing where they were being taken. One community leader left a note to "Dear lifetime buddies, pals, and friends" in which he expressed regret but no bitterness.[39]

The immediate destination was a badly built and suffocatingly hot camp at Pinedale, California, just north of Fresno. Life was painful, excruciating, and humiliating amidst sand, desert heat, discomfort, and little to do. In time, all were moved to other locations, most to a permanent camp at Minidoka, Idaho, until shortly before the war ended. Others were allowed to leave and establish new homes in more distant areas, the reunited Matsuoka family among them. After the government allowed Nisei to volunteer for military service, a number of local men enlisted in the army's segregated 442nd Regimental Combat Team, and saw battle in Italy. One of them, Kiyo Yabuki, was wounded in both legs from flying shrapnel.

When they were allowed to return to the west coast, only eleven of the sixty families came back to Bellevue. In some cases the reception was unpleasant. Homes and fields had been destroyed or wasted, and land was occupied by others. Signs and placards warned the returnees that they were unwelcome, and a mass meeting at the elementary school auditorium was aimed at keeping them away. When war hero Yabuki took his uniform to a Bellevue cleaner, he was turned away because he was a "Jap." Many of the Japanese remained in the areas where they had settled during the war; the Matsuoka family, for instance, thrived near a small town in north central Montana.[40] Those who returned gradually gained acceptance and again became respected residents of the Bellevue community. In 1993, the city dedicated four Japanese cherry trees at the new Downtown Park—reminiscent of earlier ones that had lined the street at the former high school site. In 1988 the federal government officially apologized and gave monetary compensation to the remaining evacuees.

Other Asians who made marked contributions to the area included Andrew and Marc Balatico, brothers who emigrated from The Philippines in the mid-1920s. After working for a railroad and then on several farms, Andrew Balatico leased and later purchased 23 acres off the old Mercer Slough and, with his younger brother, planted vegetables sold there and at the Pike Place Market in Seattle. He kept meticulous records in a day book. "Whole day work, whole day work," he once wrote. His daughter recalled him working for two to eight months without a single day off. Before he died in 1998, the area became a city park, but he continued to farm it and show it to school children.[41]

Later generations of Asian Americans lived and worked near those plots of land the Japanese and Filipinos had farmed, but in vastly different professions. Many of the Asian immigrants who settled in Bellevue arrived with a "higher level of literacy" than most immigrants; many had post-graduate education and professional skills.[42] Engaged in electronics, communications, and related industries, they perhaps did not know of the earlier contributions or that many were occupying the same spots where the Japanese-Americans had lived and farmed. Former Japanese farms had become the sites of Vuecrest, Newport Shores, and other residential developments, of the AT&T offices, of the Glendale Country Club, of the Safeway Distribution Center, and even portions of downtown Bellevue.[43]

The African-American population has remained small. A few individual families lived scattered about small-town Bellevue, with a small cluster in the rural surroundings that became Overlake Park in the 1960s.[44] But Bellevue was "a lily-white place," according to one 1964 high school graduate whose classmates sometimes ventured to Seattle just to meet black kids.[45] The first black to purchase a home in the newly developing Lake Hills found real estate agents and owners reluctant to sell and the family's presence became a community issue. He attributed several unpleasant incidents to "ignorance rather than malice," and the family, the only blacks in Lake Hills for at least five years, were slowly accepted.[46]

————————————

Women are not entirely absent from McDonald's account, but she stresses the men who built Bellevue. There is some irony that this woman who broke barriers in the largely male profession of journalism with stints as an overseas correspondent as early as 1920, did not say more about the women of Bellevue.

The women of the pioneer phase seem to have dutifully followed their husbands to the primitive Eastside. We learn that Aaron Mercer brought his wife Ann to their small log cabin, but then left her alone to raise their children for long periods. Clark Sturtevant probably had an Indian wife, and some of the Burrows' land holdings resulted from an inheritance Mrs. Burrows obtained. A few women took on wider roles. After her husband died in 1890, Isabel Bechtel was postmistress for several months and later handled her own forty-acre tract. And we see a photo of May Johnson on horseback as she delivered the mail along the Eastside.

Not surprisingly, early teachers were women, beginning with Calanthia Wyoming Burrows. The sixteen-year-old Florence Stowell took a teaching position in 1887, but soon lost it because a law prohibited the hiring of persons under eighteen. When the "permanent" school was built on Main Street in 1892, Adelaide Frances Mickels was its first teacher, and her successors were women. And when Bellevue finally acquired its own high school, the first two graduates were women. Women were also early telephone operators, and the daughters of W. Eugene LeHuquet helped put out the town's first newspaper, *The Reflector*, a family operation.

When women banded together in organizations, their purposes were often for social causes. McDonald does not note the part women played in establishing early churches, but they were instrumental in forming the first one, Bellevue Congregational Church, in 1896. In 1922, a group of women established a study club that soon became the Bellevue Women's Club, which endured for almost half a century. A handwritten note held by the Bellevue Historical Society gives a clue as to its founding. The Bellevue Improvement Club already existed, the anonymous informer recalled, "but all men, women wanted in but due to personalities we were not invited." Nicely printed programs detailed each year's activities, held in homes and frequently given over to talks or discussions of art, musical programs, and book reviews. But the Women's Club began to take on community issues in earnest. They helped establish a public park with a public land grant and raised funds with such events as a Fall Festival, dances, and baby beauty contests. They collected books for a library their volunteers operated at increasingly better locations over several decades, with Marguerite Groves and Jennie Clayton as longtime librarians. They took stands on public issues locally and regionally, sent funds and clothing to institutions for needy persons, and expressed concern about traffic control and schools. When they disbanded in 1971, their few remaining possessions included a piano and an American flag. The small treasury went to a program for troubled children. "I think the death of a club equally sad," commented longtime member Bertha Lysell.[47]

Larger and aimed specifically at service to needy families was the Overlake Service League. It evolved after Ruby Bilger Davis and Ida C. Curtis started a Hunts Point chapter of the Seattle Fruit and Flower Mission (later the Seattle Milk Fund) in 1911. Within a few years the members decided to create their own organization aimed at helping poorer families and children on the Eastside. "In those days daintily dressed ladies with hats and gloves offered their services directly without a caseworker." They provided clothes, meals, layettes, and convalescent robes, along with milk to school children, meals, and Christmas and Easter baskets. Additional circles were formed, with sixteen in the late 1950s, each having about 25 members. They raised funds in various ways, including a shop selling used items that still operates in the Bellevue Shopping Square in 2000.[48]

Similarly, local units of the Seattle Orthopedic Guild helped meet the needs of Seattle's children's hospital. Such organizations provided various kinds of service to individuals and groups. Bellevue women were deeply involved in the preparation and work for each Strawberry Festival, and many participated in the growing number of neighborhood community clubs. And there was the traditional involvement with broader women's and youth groups including Camp Fire Girls, Girl Scouts, Parent-Teacher organizations, and Masonic and other fraternal or sorority groups.

McDonald notes that early lists of business people included two women dressmakers and Laura Shear's life insurance office. Persons shopping along Main Street would find women working in many of the businesses, many as proprietors. Grace Sandell ran a lunchroom at the ferry dock, and Mrs. Menefee and Florence Carter had restaurants, the latter letting rooms and serving meals to men in the small whaling fleet. Clemmie Evans had a sewing shop and then a bakery; Adelaide Belote, first president of the Women's Club, was almost legendary as assistant postmistress for several generations; Elinor Whitney was the equal partner with her husband in putting out *The Bellevue American*, as was Angie LeWarne in the family's small variety store.

But no Bellevue businesswoman made a greater mark on that small community than Meta Jacobson Burrows. Fresh out of pharmacy school in 1934 she opened Meta's Drug Store in a former bank building at Main and School Streets (now 102nd NE). Meta's supplied many needs to townspeople and housed the state liquor store, but the most notable feature was "the long soda fountain counter. For youngsters a stop there was a special treat, but on those round red stools oldsters gathered to visit, gossip and doubtless conduct business and reach agreements on civic affairs. Who can know all that transpired there?"[49] A longtime business neighbor confirmed he would "never forget the buttered cinnamon rolls and green rivers," noting that many early projects in Bellevue were hatched over those cinnamon rolls. Eventually owning six other drug stores in the vicinity, Meta Burrows was arguably Bellevue's first real businesswoman. When her Main Street store closed in 1979, it was located a few doors east of its original site and was the town's oldest continuously operating business.[50]

Bellevue women, as those across the nation, were affected by World War II. Home life and routines were disrupted and wives and mothers saw loved ones leave for war. Many who had never worked outside the home took on jobs in the regular work force or at defense plants such as the Lake Washington Shipyards a few miles north or the Boeing B-29 plant at Renton. Women also handled such "home front" chores as serving on draft boards and rationing boards and they held other duties related to civil defense. Local nurses set up care centers throughout the community to be used in case of emergency. Bellevue's many Japanese-American women, of course, were moved out to concentration camps elsewhere in the West.

As Bellevue became more suburban, women became increasingly prominent in business and social and civic organizations. The Kandy Kane in the Shopping Square, where Carol Barber handled customers with brusque affection, came to take on some of the meeting place aspects of Meta's Drug Store. When Frederick & Nelson ventured beyond downtown Seattle to open its first branch store in the Square, Ruth Slater was chosen as its manager. Slater rapidly became a fixture and leader in the business community and in civic affairs. The formation of a chapter of the Business Women's and Professional Club was evidence that women were emerging from home and traditional women-focused activities to something new. This organization grew rapidly and concerned itself with helping women assume new roles in a more highly professional society and improving the general business climate. Chapters of such sororal organizations as the American Association of University Women, the League of Women Voters, and P.E.O. were also formed.

Women helped to organize the Arts and Crafts Fair, the Surrey Play Barn Theater, and later the Bellevue Art Museum and a symphony orchestra, and the Bellevue Historical Society, and thus expand the community's cultural focus. Harriet Shorts was instrumental in donating the family home and garden to create the Bellevue Botanical Garden. Women took part in garden clubs, the new yacht club and the golf club. They led organizational efforts for a community hospital along with other benefits for the community.[51] *The Bellevue American* headlined that the "Man of the Year" for 1959 was a woman, Helen Bucey, and a year later the "Outstanding Citizen," as the title was clearly designated, was Jane Wood. Both were longtime volunteers in several organizations and active in the hospital drive.[52]

Moreover, suburban Bellevue viewed women as consumers. It was perhaps not unintentional that the Square and other shopping centers were geared to automobiles where the young mother could bring her offspring nearly to the door of the store where she would shop and take them with ease through the store. And the stores themselves were more and more geared to carrying goods for women. Newly styled homes, too, emphasized the kitchen with its appliances, an open family room nearby, and ease of housekeeping.[53]

Early on women served as clerks of school boards. Borghild Ringdall of Highland became a fixture in that position and other community activities and she later headed food services for the growing school district; a school was named for her. In 1961, Dorothy Broderson became the first woman principal in modern-day Bellevue. Women increasingly served on civic boards and commissions including the city council where Nancy Rising and Margot Blacker were leaders in different periods of time. Several, such as longtime Councilwoman Georgia Zumdieck, had emerged as activists for their neighborhoods. Andrea Beatty came from Texas to become the first city manager of a sizable city. Not until 1988, however, did the city elect a woman as mayor, Nan Campbell. Meanwhile other local women were serving on the County Council and in other elective positions.

Most notable was Bellevue High graduate and Newport Shores resident Jennifer Dunn. During a long career chairing the state Republican Party, she held appointive positions with both the Reagan and Bush administrations. Then she turned to elective office and was elected to the House of Representatives in 1992, where she soon held leadership positions.

As the 21st century began, women made up just over half of the population of Bellevue and were securely prominent in civic and business leadership. When edge-city Bellevue debated its future course, a major player was Connie Grant. Her family was planning to develop a large complex of shops, restaurants, and offices on the acreage which her grandparents had farmed on the fringe of Bellevue when it was small-town.

———————————

Lucile McDonald was another of Bellevue's notable women. She continued to write into her early nineties and was anxious about plans to publish an autobiography penned years earlier. A special honor came on March 9, 1991 when Governor Booth Gardner proclaimed Lucile McDonald Day. She was also selected by the School of Journalism Hall of Fame at the University of Oregon, her alma mater. Lucile McDonald died on June 23, 1992, at the age of 93.

As a resident of the Eastside since 1944, McDonald continually wrote about Bellevue and its environs. It is noteworthy that in the year of her birth, Bellevue was a lakeshore village in which many of its pioneers still lived. It was becoming the small town it would remain for several decades. When McDonald moved to Bellevue in 1972, it was clearly a suburb of Seattle just across the lake from her home. And by the time she died it had become an urban center in its own right. Her lifetime spanned most of the history of her adopted town.

Introduction Notes

1. McDonald, Lucile, *A Foot in the Door: The Reminiscences of Lucile McDonald, with Richard McDonald*. Especially, Lorraine McConaghy, "Foreword," pp. ix–xvii (Pullman, WA: Washington State University Press, 1995; McConaghy, "Introduction and Acknowledgements," in Lorraine McConaghy, editor, *Lucile McDonald's Eastside Notebook: 101 Local History Vignettes* (Redmond, WA: Marymoor Museum, 1993), pp. 1–11. See the McConaghy pieces for a reliable critique of McDonald as historian.

2. Charles P. LeWarne, "Bellevues I Have Known: Reflections on the Evolution of an 'Edge City,'" *Columbia: The Magazine of Northwest History*," 11:3–4 (Summer, 1997).

3. On names, see T. T. Waterman, "The Geographical Names Used by the Indians of the Pacific Coast," *The Geographical Review*, 12:175–94 (January 1922).

4. David M. Buerge, "Indian Lake Washington," *The Weekly* (Seattle), August 1–7, 1984, pp. 29–33 , and "The Eastside's Forgotten War," *Eastsideweek*, July 12, 1995, pp. 12–17 (quotations, pp. 16, 17).

5. Schmid, Calvin F., and Stanton E. Schmid, *Growth of Cities and Towns: State of Washington* (Olympia, WA: Washington State Community and Affairs Agency, 1969), pp. 41, 69–70.

6. LeWarne, "Bellevues," p. 5.

7. Ibid., p. 6.

8. Robert F. Karolevitz, *Kemper Freeman, Sr. and the Bellevue Story* (Mission Hill, SD: The Homestead Publishers, 1984) is a biography that also relates much of the history of Bellevue.

9. *The Bellevue American*, August 15, 1946.

10. LeWarne, "Bellevues," p. 6.

11. "Bellevue, Washington," undated promotional brochure in Bellevue Historical Society collection.

12. *The Bellevue American*, July 23, 1959.

13. Hilltop's history is described by a founder in Victor B. Scheffer, *Hilltop: A Collaborative Community* (Bellevue: Bellevue Historical Society, 1994).

14. This account of Lake Hills is based on Lorraine McConaghy, *No Ordinary Place: Three Postwar Suburbs and Their Critics*. Ph. D. dissertation, University of Washington, 1993.

15. Ibid., p. 298.

16. Rillmond Schear, "The Great Big Boom in Bellevue," *Seattle Magazine*, 2:28–37, 45–47 (June 1965), quotation, p. 29. One such "plastic" reference was in *The Daily Journal-American* (Bellevue), February 21, 1979.

17. Joel Garreau, *Edge City: Life on the New Frontier* (New York, London, Toronto, Sydney, and Auckland: Anchor Books, Doubleday, 1991).

18. As summarized in LeWarne, "Bellevues," p. 9.

19. Garreau, *Edge City*, 436. The nearby I-405 and the Mercer Island and east I-90 corridors were listed as "emerging edge cities" along with South Center [sic] and the Kent Valley. Vancouver-Clark County were not listed as an edge city of Portland, Oregon. p. 435. Garreau concedes his list may not be complete.

20. Federal and state census reports.

21. City of Bellevue, *Bellevue Chronicles, 1863–1992* (Bellevue, ca. 1992).

22. Described by Peter Armato, April 21, 2000.

23. Bert McNae, with Nancy Way, *The Bert McNae Story: Vision Guts & Money*, quotation, p. 103 (Redmond, WA, 1995).

24. *The Seattle Times Northwest 100*, (supplement), June 1, 1999 (quotation, p. G2).

25. City of Bellevue, *Bellevue Environmental Scan* (Bellevue: City of Bellevue Department of Planning and Community Development, 1999), p. EC-1.

26. Quotation from *The Seattle Times*, December 5, 1994, p. A-1.

27. City of Bellevue, *Bellevue Environment Scan*, pp. EC-10–11.

28. *Seattle Post-Intelligencer*, October 18, 1994, pp. A-1, A-4.

29. Bellevue School District, *District and School Profiles, 1997–98*, p. 18.

30. City of Bellevue, *Bellevue Environment Scan*, p. ED-6, ED-5, DE-1. It should be noted that the Bellevue School District is not completely contiguous with the city limits and that enrollment in private schools is on the rise.

31. United States Department of Commerce, Bureau of the Census, *1990 Census of Population and Housing* (Washington: U.S. Government Printing Office, 1991), 23, 20. These figures do not take into account the increasing numbers of persons who consider themselves multi-racial.

32. City of Bellevue, *Bellevue Environment Scan*, p. DE-19.

33. Ibid., PS-4, 5.

34. Quoted in Richard W. Larsen, *Eastside Story*, n.p.: [Eastside Leadership Committee], ca. 1997, p. 12.

35. City of Bellevue, *Bellevue Environment Scan*, p. TR-1.

36. Ibid., pp. CV-1, 2, "1997 Community Values Survey."

37. Richard E. Berner, *Seattle in the 20th Century, Vol. 3: Seattle Transformed, World War II to Cold War* (Seattle: Charles Press, 1999), p. 18.

38. The following account is based in large part on a series of articles by David Neiwert that appeared in the *Journal-American* between May 10 and May 31, 1992, the fiftieth anniversary of the evacuation of Bellevue's Japanese-Americans. A manuscript by Asaichi Tsushima, "Pre-WWII History of Japanese Pioneers in the Clearing and Development of Land in Bellevue," 1952, is in the Bellevue Historical Society. A manuscript by Joseph R. Svinth, "Getting a Grip: Judo in the Japanese American Communities of Washington and Oregon, Circa 1900–Circa 1950," is in the King County Landmarks and Heritage Program office, Seattle. Communication with Alice Ito, May 11, 2000.

39. *Bellevue American*, May 21, 1942.

40. *Montana Farmer-Stockman*, November 3, 1966.

41. *The Seattle Times*, December 13, 1998; see also, November 7, 1971.

42. City of Bellevue, *Bellevue Environment Scan*, pp. DE-19, DE-9.

43. *Journal-American*, May 31, 1992, p. A8.

44. Bert McNae, *The Bert McNae Story*, pp. 132–36.

45. *The Seattle Times*, June 26, 1994, p. A-13.

46. Harold Martin interview by Lorraine McConaghy, February 18, 1992, typescript in Bellevue Historical Society.

47. Bellevue Women's Club folders in Bellevue Historical Society.

48. *History of Overlake Service League, 1911–1959*, in Bellevue Historical Society.

49. LeWarne, "Bellevues," p. 4.

50. *Journal-American*, September 3, 1979, p. A3.

51. Lorraine McConaghy presents a summary of the somewhat differing activities of women in Bellevue and in Lake Hills in *No Ordinary Place*, pp. 298–300.

52. *The Bellevue American*, January 28, 1960, and January 26, 1961.

53. One Lake Hills builder specifically noted homes intended to please women; see Lorraine McConaghy, *No Ordinary Place*, p. 282.

BELLEVUE

ITS FIRST 100 YEARS

Original text

IT WAS ALMOST A CENTURY AGO [written in 1984] that Bellevue was given its name and began its slow growth—slow until completion of the first Lake Washington bridge in 1940 sent a stream of population flowing toward the Eastside.

In writing the history of Bellevue one must keep in mind that the city shares boundaries with several other municipalities. Many persons with a Bellevue address or telephone number actually live in Clyde Hill, Beaux Arts, Medina, Hunts Point, Yarrow, Newcastle or in King County. This account will stay as much as possible strictly inside the city limits.

At the time of its incorporation in 1953 Bellevue covered slightly less than six square miles and had a population of 5,950. Today it sprawls over 24.5 square miles, its northeast section touches Lake Sammamish and its southern boundary takes in high land east of (but not including) Factoria and a strip of lakeshore south of Highway 90 reaching Pleasure Point. The population is approaching 80,000.

Though it is the fourth largest city in the state, its development for many years was slower than that of other communities east of Lake Washington. Its shopping center for food and farm supplies was at Midlakes and when families wanted anything else they generally took a day off and went to Seattle. Some of the pioneer settlers, after expending effort in rowing, had a long walk home with sacks of necessities on their backs. In bad weather they often had to seek an overnight refuge before covering the entire distance. If fog overtook them they sometimes had to paddle all night to keep warm. Winters were colder when the lake was largely surrounded by forests and once, in 1875, ice is reported to have covered the water eight to ten inches thick.

A few men worked in the city for money to improve their land and the women and children were left on the widely scattered farms, knowing that cougars and bears inhabited the surrounding timber.

It was not Indian country, though white settlers saw canoes passing along the lake and William Meydenbauer alleged that tribesmen stole windows from his cabin when he was not there. A pair of longhouses once stood near Yarrow Bay, but the only ones inside present Bellevue were at Wilburton. Documents filed in an Indian land-claim hearing indicated that two longhouses used to be situated at the eastern tip of Mercer Slough, the place being known as Sa-tma-tal. A researcher located it north of Highway 90 in the vicinity of 118th Avenue SE and says that during the Indian war of 1855–56 marauding warriors from central Washington found refuge and stored supplies there.[1]

All of Bellevue was so heavily wooded that landseekers passed it by. It lacked trails and the only sheltered indentations were the bay and the slough. What land was acquired was mostly for speculative purposes either by timbermen or because until 1873 it was thought the Northern Pacific Railroad might build its terminus in Seattle.

The First Homesteaders

Meydenbauer and Aaron Mercer, the initial settlers of Bellevue, both staked land a few months apart, the former in March, the latter in August, 1869, but remained only long enough to prove up on their homesteads. Their log cabins are thought to have been the only ones then on

Bellevue's "first citizens," Aaron and Ann Mercer, filed a claim in 1863 on an inlet of the east shore of Lake Washington. It came to be known as Mercer Slough. The Mercer Family

the eastern shore. So few persons lived on the Eastside in 1870 that a single election precinct was established, embracing all the settlements from Black River to the mouth of the Sammamish.

Meydenbauer, a Seattle baker recently arrived from Germany, was a part-time occupant of a crude waterfront dwelling until his title was assured. His land, south of Main Street and reaching from Bellevue Way to the lake, partially surrounded a marsh when the water level was approximately nine feet higher than present.[2] After construction of the Lake Washington Ship Canal, the surface receded and condominiums now stand where ducks floated on the water in Meydenbauer's day. By 1879 he already had sold half of his 40 acres and four years later John R. Kinnear,[3] Seattle attorney, became owner of the remainder. Meydenbauer's bakery business had grown to such an extent that he wanted only a summer home site on the Eastside. Later when he sought to buy back a small piece, values had risen to $75.00 an acre and he thought this too high. Instead, he bought a lot on Hunts Point, where he erected a vacation cottage in 1906, the year he died.

Aaron Mercer's homestead was along the west side of Mercer Slough, reaching from the lake on the south to SE 24th Street on the north and inland to 112th Avenue SE. He had eight children when he built his cabin (eventually there were 11) and its furnishings were so meager that the youngsters took turns eating with the iron knives and forks at the dinner table. The family lost a baby, Tommy, who drowned in the slough before his 11-year old sister Frances could reach him.

Mercer moved in 1871 to the Duwamish Valley where his children could attend school. He sold the Bellevue property after receiving his homestead patent the following year. His cabin was still standing well into the 1880s.

While much has been written about other members of the Mercer family whose activities centered on Seattle, little has come down to us concerning those who lived in the lonely clearing beside the slough. Aaron's descendants relate only one incident in that connection. He left his wife, Ann, alone with the children much of the time and in his absence on several occasions she heard sounds as though someone were fumbling with the cabin door. When she summoned courage to look out no one was there.

But just at dusk one day, when she hears the sound again, Aaron was returning. As he approached the cabin he saw a large cougar in front of the door. Mercer shot the animal on the spot with his rifle.[4]

Mercer Slough was nine feet deeper in those days and the swamp along the lakeshore commenced well south of the mouth of Coal Creek and extended up the slough as far as present Main Street. Other breaks in the forest were bogs in the general area of Phantom and Larsen Lakes, where wild cranberries grew in abundance.

Early loggers did not like to operate more than a mile inland because of the difficulty in dragging logs out by ox team, Other settlers had not yet arrived in Bellevue and a dense stand of timber separated the land claims of Mercer and Meydenbauer. The next person on the scene was a loner, Clark M. Sturtevant, a Civil War veteran who took advantage of the law granting former service men 160 acres as a reward for their part in the conflict. In 1873 he paddled up Mercer Slough and is said to have broken seven beaver dams on the way. The property he selected lay between SE and NE 8th Streets and from 112th to 116th Avenues SE. At first he made his living by trapping, and one year marketed 130 mink pelts, four otter and a number of muskrats. Two years after acquiring his original piece of land, he bought part of the trace surrounding a lake which was named after Sturtevant. The land around the lake had been claimed by Angus and Elizabeth Mackintosh in 1872. Like a large percentage of the first land claimants, Mackintosh was another Civil War veteran who came to Seattle in 1870 and was active in real estate and investments. He founded the Merchants National Bank (in Seattle), of which he was president, and apparently his interest in the Eastside was purely speculative. He suffered financial reverses in 1895 and died in 1904. The remainder of Mackintosh's Lake Sturtevant property was sold to John and

Clark M. Sturtevant in his Civil War garb. Photo courtesy of Marymoor Museum

Agnes Sims in 1878. Sims was from Tennessee. The lake's name never formally changed, but when apartments and other building went up in 1978, the principal developer preferred to call this location Lake Bellevue.

Sturtevant lived on the site of the present city hall until his health failed and he moved to Seattle, where he acquired more property. In 1883, when he was 43, he married a 17-year-old niece of President Grover Cleveland. After her husband's death at the age of 71, Florence Sturtevant remarried and became Mrs. Hastings. At that time the family still owned the sites of the City Hall and Holiday Inn. Rumor had it that Sturtevant previously had an Indian wife, who died and was buried near his house. One informant claimed to have seen her tombstone in the yard.

A story is told of Sturtevant's bachelor years. Young Albert Selden Burrows paid him a visit and was invited to stay to lunch.

"Father looked at the table doubtfully," Burrows' son related. "It was very dirty. 'Oh, I'll clean that off,' Sturtevant said. He got a plane and planed the top."

The lakeshore near the mouth of Mercer Slough when the water level was much higher. Logging had been done before this picture, looking toward Mercer Landing, was taken.

What Mercer Slough was like early in the present century was described by an old Seattle resident. "When I was a boy, a friend and I paddled through the cattails, tules and lily pads and several species of long marsh grass. In some places we had to push the canoe across shallow spots. Other places the water was four or five feet deep and in these spots we found several muskrat houses. Near the north end we found a beaver house. We went to Mercer Slough only on Saturdays and set our traps, returning on Sundays to check them. We had to make our haul-ups, using old pieces of wood anchored with weights and copper wire and baited with carrots and pieces of apple. We caught as many as 300 muskrats a year, some bringing $2.25 each. We caught a few mink besides.

"Mercer Slough was such a wonderful place we went back in summer and camped, fishing for trout and keeping a record of the waterfowl we saw. Once a green heron was caught in one of our traps and I mounted the bird and gave it to our high school. Hundreds of ducks and geese stopped at Mercer Slough; it was the finest part of Lake Washington.

The very oldest maps show two additional land grants within Bellevue's city limits, both to prominent Seattleites. Henry Yesler in 1876 received a patent to a tract opposite Mercer's on the east side of the slough and David Denny in 1877 claimed acreage north of the central shopping district. These men never were identified with Bellevue history. Their interest must have been purely speculative. Earlier than the foregoing was a claim that scarcely seems to have been in Bellevue. It was one which Clarence Bagley staked in 1867 at Newport Shores.

Among other elusive early settlers at Bellevue in the 1870s was said to have been a man concerning whom no documentary evidence appears to exist. Albert Meydenbauer some years ago wrote that his father spoke of a retired sea captain named Allen who occupied a claim near the mouth of Mercer Slough (presumably on the side toward Factoria) and raised vegetables. He rowed to Leschi in order to take them to market in Seattle, While digging a well, the story goes, he chanced upon a seam of coal and from then on produced enough fuel for his cooking needs.[5] Evidently he became ill, took to his bed and died there. Because he had no neighbors, his body was not found until an acquaintance came to inquire about him.

Permanent Settlers

Two other men who took land and remained to farm it were L. Peterson and John Zwiefelhofer. Peterson had a log home on the present site of the Unigard complex and was the earliest recorded settler in that area. He became a poultry raiser and his family was still living on the farm in 1920.

Zwiefelhofer, an Austrian cabinetmaker who migrated to the United States in 1860, settled in 1879 on 124 acres west of the intersection of 124th Avenue NE and south of Northup Way, near the present Safeway distribution center. He had four children and when his first wife died he sent away for a widow, married and had one more child. At first Zwiefelhofer made trips to the city to work, going back and forth weekends by way of Northup Landing on Yarrow Bay. (Several farms had been started in the valley south of Houghton in the late 1870s.) While he was away his wife often plowed their land with an ox team. The husband was next employed as a powder man for the county road department. He also did dynamiting jobs in the Eastside, especially for land clearing. He grew strawberries on his own property. Zwiefelhofer later purchased the Alonzra Hefner land claim, which was homesteaded and he received title in 1885.

It is impossible to write about Bellevue's beginnings without mentioning an Irishman, Patrick Downey, whose property became Vuecrest. The only persons ahead of him in the vicinity were the King brothers of Groat Point (now in Medina), William Meydenbauer and Clark Sturtevant. Mathew and Lucien Sharp arrived a few months later.

Timber was dense on the slope where Downey built his log cabin at about 101st Avenue NE and NE 12th Street in 1882. He married 11 years later and raised 13 children. In 1896 he built a more commodious house which is still standing on NE 13th though its appearance has been greatly altered. He engaged in growing strawberries for market and operated a dairy.

Settlement of Bellevue began in earnest with the arrival in 1882 of Albert S. Burrows, Isaac Bechtel and the twin Sharp brothers. Lucien Sharp chose land south of Main Street, and between Bellevue Way and 112th Avenue SE.

Albert Burrows (1837–1896).
Rody Burrows Collection

The Burrows cabin was originally located at the foot of SE 15th near the lake. It was moved to the southwest corner of Bellevue Way and NE 8th, where this picture was taken in 1946. Shortly afterward it was moved again to 112th Avenue NE. Rody Burrows Collection

Mathew Sharp's land was between Main and NE 8th Street and 108th Avenue NE and 110th Avenue NE, which took in a large part of the future business center. (Another brother, James Sharp, arrived on the scene later.)

These men were followed in 1883 by William Sharpe (no relation to the twins) on Pickle Point, south of the entrance to Meydenbauer Bay. He was said by an oldtimer to have been a remittance man from New York who was well educated. A deed showed that his property was next acquired by Clement Sharpe of Brooklyn, N.Y. (evidently in 1884). No other record of William has been uncovered. His tract became the Shoreland district and was one of the first areas platted in Bellevue.

Another 1883 settler was Henry Thode at Phantom Lake, followed the next year by Alvin Goff at Highland and Hans Miller at Robinswood Park. Thode was not the original owner at Phantom Lake. Samuel Todd in February 1883 purchased a section of public land and divided it in tracts, the boundaries of which joined in the center of the lake and made that 63 acre body of water privately owned. Six months later he sold 160 acres to Thode, who married soon thereafter. It is said he was then five miles from his nearest neighbor. The Thodes lived in a log cabin, raised pota-toes, and kept cows, sheep, turkeys, ducks and geese. Pheasants and grouse were plentiful around the place and bears were often seen.

Thode distinguished himself by digging single-handedly a new out-let for the lake, causing it to drain the swamps toward Lake Sammamish instead of into Kelsey Creek. Early some mornings a pillar of fog used to come up this new channel where there is a drop in elevation of about 220 feet. The vapor seemed to take the shape of a human profile approach-ing from the east. When it got over the lake it faded and this phenom-enon inspired the name of Phantom. Originally it was called Beaver Lake.

The city's oldest structure on its original site is the Hans Miller cabin in Robinswood Park. Built in 1884, this is how it looked before age and weather took their toll. Miller erected a log barn the following year. City of Bellevue

The Daniel W. Frazier cabin, erected in 1888, was moved to Kelsey Creek Park in 1974. It is one of Bellevue's few remaining pioneer structures. Harriet N. Watters

Henry Thode became mentally ill in 1894 and was sent to the state hospital, where he died two years later. His widow married Jacob Kamber, a Swiss who settled at the lake. Three other German-speaking residents obtained land on its border. Alwyn Berndt bought 30 acres of the Thode property in 1907 where the present Boeing Data Center now stands. (His son, Otto, later acquired 160 acres.) It had been logged two years earlier. Alwyn Berndt, himself a tree-topper, saw so much downed timber going to waste around there he thought the residents of Bellevue must be exceedingly lazy. His other neighbors were the Ahrendt and Herman Gube families. Gube lived 14 years at Phantom Lake, dying in 1924 as the result of being injured by a mad cow.

Thode's daughter, Helen, was the first white child born in Bellevue (in 1886). She married Albert Boddy of Hunts Point.

The Need for a School

Providing a school for their children was among the initial considerations of the several settlers near Bellevue's waterfront and the effort to do so fostered the birth of the community. Albert Burrows was a carpenter who had fought in several battles of the Civil War and was entitled to a soldier's homestead. He came from Des Moines, Iowa in 1882, spending 21 days on the journey by train and boat. He started working for a Seattle sawmill, but having the urge to find land for himself, got in touch with George Miller, who had taken a homestead at Beaux Arts in 1883 and was most anxious to have a family with children living near him so as to justify organizing a school for his own offspring. He showed Burrows a tract of lake frontage at Killarney which had not yet been claimed and the latter staked the 160 acres and built a log cabin.[6] Later he constructed a more palatial house with gingerbread scrollwork and trim and some windows edged in colored glass.

Burrows often worked in Seattle, staying away many days at a time

Albert S. Burrows' second home in Bellevue built in the 1880s The woman in the hat is Calanthia Burrows, Bellevue's first teacher. Rody Burrows Collection, photo courtesy of Marymoor Museum

Jesse B. Warren (1839–1913)
Photo courtesy of Marymoor Museum

and rowing home. He served in the 1894 legislature and died two years afterward of bronchitis. His son, Albert Selden Burrows, born in 1871, received only 30 months of regular schooling, but continued to educated himself and was a member of the University of Washington's first graduating class. At times he was absent because he worked at logging. When he completed his course he taught at Tolt, riding there from Bellevue on a horse in order to secure the appointment. He taught in 1898 in Bellevue, and in 1905 he became King County's superintendent of schools.

Haying on the Jesse Warren farm, part of present Bellevue Square. Warren is beside the wagon and his son-in-law, Alex Gordon, is driving. Rody Burrows Collection

A 1900 view of Warren property close to NE 8th and 100th where the Crabapple Restaurant stood in Bellevue Square. Rody Burrows Collection

Mrs. Burrows inherited the property of a bachelor, Zina Van Duzen, 80 acres just south of Miller's and reaching to the point near the present East Channel Bridge. She had taken care of this neighbor before he died of pneumonia. Her son took charge of Van Duzen's burial and Selden's mother gave him the land. Van Duzen was remembered by the pioneer settlers as "a thin man who used flour sacks for socks."

Albert Selden Burrows married the daughter of Jesse B. Warren, who in 1891 purchased 25 acres of the Mathew Sharp estate on the square. This was where the big madrona tree stood that in modern times was a landmark in front of the Crabapple Restaurant. (Nordstrom's is there now.)

Warren, originally from Northern Ireland, had lived in the Dakotas before coming to Bellevue in 1890. He joined the Washington Produce and Fruit Growers Union and his grandson, Rody Burrows, owned an identifying button which a member going to the city to sell produce was given in 1895 upon payment of 10 cents, in order to obtain a stall for the day.

The elder Burrows' closest neighbor was Isaac Bechtel, a Swiss from Ontario, Canada. Leaving behind his wife and six children in March 1882, he went to California, where he worked several months at logging before

May Johnson, born in Prussia, was 41 when she carried mail from Houghton to Bellevue twice a week from 1895 to 1896 for $50 a year. Photo courtesy of Marymoor Museum

boarding a ship for Seattle. In August he learned of 129 acres of unclaimed land with three-fourths of a mile of waterfront, which he filed on as a preemption, paying the government 23 cents an acre for it. He built a cabin immediately, with the help of Pat Downey, whose homestead was directly north of him. Bechtel set out a cherry and apple orchard and did some logging, which soon was to make a great alteration in Bellevue's landscape. After living alone for a while, he borrowed enough money to send to Canada for the other members of his family. They arrived in Seattle in August, 1885, walked through the woods to the lake and were rowed across to their new home.

Logging the Square

Isaac Bechtel, Jr. recalled, "The Eastside was just a vast stretch of timber with only a few cabins showing. Our nearest neighbors were the bachelors, Matt and Lucien Sharp, who homesteaded where much of the present Bellevue shopping center is located. For the next four years my father operated a small logging camp employing a few men and my two oldest brothers. They used as many as six ox teams and a wooden track. They logged the central area almost to Highway 405, also Pat Downey's homestead at Vuecrest and much of Medina. Meydenbauer Bay was so full of logs one could almost walk across it. Rafts were made up and towed to the Phinney mill on the west shore.

"Logging was a hard life. I remember in 1907 we thought we were getting a tremendous price when logs went to $10.00 a thousand. They had been as low as 10 cents per thousand or 10 cents per cord. Settlers were glad when the trees were cut. You could bootleg timber on unoccupied property and never hear a complaint about it."

The size of some of the trees that grew near Bellevue Square can be judged by the one that stood near NE 8th Street measuring 325 feet in height and nine feet in diameter.

Bechtel went on to say, "My father was the first postmaster. Bellevue was named in 1886 when a designation was needed for both the school and post office." (Bechtel's statement could apply only to the post office. The school appears to have been named several years earlier. An 1880 map of King County shows only three communities on the Eastside—Juanita, Houghton and Newcastle. The territorial census of 1887 listed Bellevue residents as living in Newcastle.)

Previously Matt Sharp had gone to Houghton once a week and brought mail from there. It was distributed at a primitive grocery his brother opened on Main Street. Matt died at the age of 31 and Bechtel took over the postal duties, his cabin becoming the post office in July, 1886. He had purchased a sailboat from William Easter, of Yarrow Point and went every Saturday to Seattle for the mail, carrying it to the lake on his back and sailing across.

The elder Bechtel was killed when he got caught in a log jam while unloading timber near Wildwood Park on November 14, 1890, and his widow, Isabel, carried on the duties of the postmistress the following year. She lived on the homestead at Lochleven for ten years and was popular with her neighbors. Lacking an adequate water supply, the women used to gather on the beach below her house every Monday morning to do their

Mrs. Isabel Bechtel with two daughters at their home in Lochleven which served as postoffice. This building was at NE 12th and Bellevue Way. Photo courtesy of Marymoor Museum

laundry and Mrs. Bechtel would bring them tea. Eventually she lost title to the property because of outstanding bills against it when her husband died. The family did not leave Bellevue, but moved to a 40 acre tract she bought from David James Shiach. Mrs. Bechtel was a doughty Scotswoman, very resourceful and much respected. When she retired as postmistress in 1891 William Ivey succeeded her and served for 23 years as postmaster.

When Ivey came to Bellevue from Seattle he arranged with the *City of Latona*[7] to bring his family and household goods across the lake. The latter were piled in a scow attached to the side of the boat. His daughter wrote: "We children sat and looked at it. There was all of our furniture, piano, three cows, one horse, a crate of chickens, two pigs, a dog and a cat."

Ivey became justice of the peace as well as postmaster, notary and insurance agent.

Who named Bellevue?

Turning back again to 1883 when the first school was built, Albert Burrows and George Miller[8] towed a raft of lumber six miles from the Phinney sawmill and erected a 10-by-12 foot shanty of upright boards on

Burrows' land. Its blackboard was comprised of three 12-inch boards, four feet long, assembled in a corner of the room. Three home-made seats accommodated two children each and a desk was constructed for the teacher. It is said that Lucien Sharp furnished the windows, asking no payment except the privilege of selecting a name for the school. The Sharps came from Indiana and somewhere in the East was another Bellevue with which Lucien had pleasant associations.

Two other versions of the naming of Bellevue differ from this. One states that William T. Sharpe and two other men were on the south point of Meydenbauer Bay when they heard hammering nearby and got in a rowboat to see what was going on. When they learned that a school was under construction Sharpe offered the windows for it in exchange for the naming privilege. One of his companions was Ed Downing, who was inspired by the name of Bellevue, Ohio.

The third version credits the name with originating when two postal inspectors called on the widow Bechtel and declared that her post office needed a proper designation. Thereupon, they settled on Bellevue because of the attractive view from her house overlooking the lake.

However it came about, the community now had an official identity, and has kept the name ever since.

School Opens

School opened in 1883 (in Killarney near 108th Avenue SE and SE 25th Street) with Calanthia Burrows (who earned $40 per three-month period) as the first teacher. Of its seven pupils, five were Millers and two were Burrows. Calanthia married Charles Meyers, who does not appear to have owned land on the Eastside. She and her husband moved to Capitol Hill in Seattle; he went into real estate and also worked for the county. He died in 1920, Calanthia in 1930.

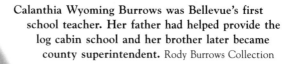

Calanthia Wyoming Burrows was Bellevue's first school teacher. Her father had helped provide the log cabin school and her brother later became county superintendent. Rody Burrows Collection

By the time the second school year was to open the Olds family with two children was established on the east shore of Mercer Island. To make it easier for them to attend, it was decided to hold classes in a cabin near the present east end of the East Channel Bridge. H.E. Kelsey was the teacher, with nine pupils enrolled.

Kelsey, a bachelor recently arrived from New York, arranged to board with the Olds, sleep in their loft and row their children back and forth to school. One November day the wind was wild and the boat swamped. Olds had to rescue the youngsters. Mrs. Olds refused to let them go again by boat and Kelsey wanted no more dunking in the lake. The pupils from the Bellevue side already had quit and the parents agreed to divide the term in half, so that classes would be held two months on Mercer Island and two months at Bellevue. Kelsey thenceforth lived at the school, the Olds children were taught by their mother and only the Millers crossed the channel to attend the full term.

Kelsey bought 160 acres in 1888 from the Northern Pacific Railroad, the center of the tract being near the present intersection of NE 8th and 140th Avenue NE. Kelsey Creek crossed his land and the city park is named for him.[9] Kelsey married and began selling portions of the property. In a few years he moved to Hawaii where he became well known as an educator.

Attendance at the Bellevue school increased in 1886 when another move was made to a small shack in a berry field north of where the

Catholic Church was later built. The school was then on the Noe Lanier farm, an 80 acre tract he acquired in 1883 north of Main Street and between Matt Sharp's and Sturtevant's land claims. (Lanier, a Seattle contractor, was born in Quebec and was absent some years from his farm during the Klondike and Alaska gold rushes.)

This time the six months term ran through the summer and the teacher was H.C. Jeffrey, a lawyer, who permitted the pupils to study in a grove of large trees just beyond the fence while he sweltered indoors hearing recitations. When it came time to change to another class he rapped on the wall to summon the children.

The Final School Site

The next quarters of the school, after its fourth move, was a new one-room board and batten cabin. The 16-by-20 foot structure was a short distance from the lake on a 200 foot square lot on Main Street, donated by John Kinnear solely for this purpose. This was in 1887 and that October Miss Florence Stowell, a graduate of Seattle High School, barely past her sixteenth birthday, was the teacher. She had eight pupils, five from the Bechtel family. She recalled, "I received $30 a month and paid $10 board. I was rich."

In 1888 another teacher, Carrie B. Lake, had to be secured for Bellevue because of a new territorial law prohibiting hiring one under 18 years of age. Others who followed here were Mrs. Annie Houghton Blakney[10] and Mrs. Mary Raine (1891).

Until Washington became a state in 1889, schools had to be supported by the communities, but the change in government permitted tax levies for this purpose. Bellevue's first bond for erecting a school was issued in January 1892 and signed by members of the initial school board consisting of Burrows, J.B. Warren and A.H. Seely, with W.E. Conway as

This school was erected on present Main Street. It began with two rooms and a bell tower and in 1892 the right section was added. Originally a large outhouse stood in the rear yard. Today a Chevron gas station occupies the site at Main Street and 100th Avenue SE. Alan Sharpe

the clerk. Their purpose was to replace the flimsy cabin with a substantial building on the same site. In 1892 a two-room structure with a bell tower went up to the east of its predecessor. It cost $1500 and Bechtel, Burrows, Meyers, Sturtevant and Downey were employed on the construction. The first three comprised the next year's school board and Lucien Sharp was clerk. The teacher was Adelaide Frances Mickels.

To this school came children from Clyde Hill, Beaux Arts and Medina, walking as much as two miles through the woods to get there. At first, the Goff children from the Highland District lived too far from the Bellevue school and there was no road to it, so they walked to Houghton, which had the oldest school on the Eastside.

Three More Schools

Another school opened in 1887 in a log shack where a Scottish settler, Matt Murdoch, had intended to live near the present Bellevue-

Redmond Road. He changed his mind and sold the place to William Shiach. The structure became the first Highland School, the parents laying a floor of split cedar. They drove spikes in the wall for hanging coats, and John Zwiefelhofer fashioned a table for the teacher, Daniel Collins, who boarded at the John Sanderson home. Classes opened that fall with 13 students enrolled, among them the Goff children. The building, situated on the south side NE 24th near 140th NE, was replaced in 1912 with a better one, topped with a big bell that served as a timekeeper for the neighborhood.

Once several children attending the earlier building encountered a forest fire on the way home. It was burning on both sides of the road. The older girls grabbed the hands of the little ones and dashed up a hill for safety.

Highland was followed in 1890 by a third school at Northup. Miss Margaret Yarno, of Seattle, related that she taught there in 1893, traveling to Madison Park by stage, boarding a boat bound for Curtis Landing on Yarrow Bay and walking the rest of the way. She went home only on weekends.

Confusion prevails about Bellevue's next school because of the name given it, but when records are checked for District 117 it becomes clear that the designation belongs both to the Mercer Slough and Phantom Lake schools; one is the predecessor of the other. The log cabin not far east of the present Eastgate fire station on 147th SE came first. Why it was associated with the slough is not known, unless it was named because it was located beside the trail to that body of water. (A modern property development in the same area also took that name.) Settlers petitioned for the school in December 1893 and it started early the following year in an abandoned bachelor's cabin in a clearing.

Helen Thode Boddy related that she and her sister walked two miles by trail from their father's farm at Phantom Lake to attend. "The cracks

Beaux Arts, Bellevue School District 49, September 1911. Palmer G. Lewis

between the floor boards were so wide the skunks used to come up and look for crumbs when we ate our lunch," she said. "We had no Chic Sale, (outhouse), so the boys went to the woods on one side and the girls on the other. Our teacher was very much afraid of bears."

Paul Heaton, another of the 1893 pupils, recalled, "The day school started I carried my chair on my back to the cabin. All the children had to bring chairs from home. The long desks were nailed to the wall and we sat facing it, with the teacher sitting behind us at his desk. This was a situation not much to our liking. Later the directors put a small window in the roof for more light. When strong winds blew I could see large trees bending over it as if they were about to fall on the school."

The children that first year were two Thodes, three Heatons and Tom Bagley. Their parents were the school directors and Mrs. W.H. Heaton was clerk. Attendance increased little by little and evidently the cabin was enlarged (possibly around 1911) although it was still only one room. By then it was definitely known as the Phantom Lake School. In 1917 it moved into a new building at 14831 SE 16th, where it remained until it was closed in 1942, having been consolidated with the Bellevue district.

The Population Grows

It is difficult to discover names of all the newcomers who moved to Bellevue. Even before Matt Sharp died in 1886, the twin brothers had been parting with some of their land, for they had a habit of deeding pieces of acreage in payment for their board. Neither of them was married and it is said their aunt, Diantha Noble, at times kept house for them.

Mrs. Noble and her husband, James, in 1889 paid $200 for a 40-acre tract of Northern Pacific land lying between Main and NE 5th Streets, and 120th and 124th Avenues NE Later their household goods were brought in on the first train to Bellevue. Noble was a Civil War veteran.

Lucien Sharp was still in Bellevue in 1900. His older brother, James, who took land in 1885, had a wife and two daughters.

Records show that James Orme arrived in 1882 and in 1884 Hans Miller, a Dane, erected a log cabin at the present Robinswood Park. Both it and a second larger log house that he built in 1895 are still to be seen on the grounds. The former is now Bellevue's oldest building on the original site. The later house was modernized in 1940 by Judge William J. Wilkins after it had stood vacant 15 years. Richard Lang was the last private owner, living there about 20 years and turning it into an elaborate country estate. When he moved to Seattle, the City of Bellevue used money from a 1970 bond issue to buy 45 acres for a park.

Alvin and Mary Goff built a two story log house on the 120-acre homestead they took in the Highland district in 1884. Some of the structure is still in use, though moved to another location on West Sammamish Way. When new it was deep in the timber and Goff had to open a skid road to it, using on ox team. He squared the large logs by hand and hoisted them in place with pulleys. Goff, a wagonmaker, met Mary in California. Her parents had crossed the plains by wagon train, and he had come by way of the Isthmus of Panama. Descendants of the couple tell of the first winter in the log house when much snow fell and drafts blew through the inadequate chinking of the walls. The only heat was from a kitchen stove. Goff was frequently ill, blaming the dampness for his poor health. He lived only eight years after coming to the Eastside. Mary remained in the same house until her death in 1939, close to her 92nd birthday.

Mrs. Goff's sister, Ann Dunn, and her husband, Roscoe, had an adjoining homestead. One of the Goff daughters (they had eight children) was married in 1895 in the log house. A Baptist minister, who was also a dentist and something of a doctor, rode horseback from Kirkland to perform the ceremony.

Mrs. Dunn kept the Northup post office, which she named for a pioneer family near Yarrow Bay. Her house was adjacent to 116th Avenue NE and Northup Way. The farm tract, straddling Highway 405, was annexed to Bellevue in 1972. Northup community once had, in addition to the school, a small store and was a stop on the railroad, an old box car serving as its station.

Trails Become Roads

One of the oldest roads on the Eastside, begun in 1879, reached from the lake to Northup and eventually was extended out NE 24th Street. Roads did not pass through Bellevue, but rather around it. They avoided bogs and other wetlands, leaving such areas to hunters of birds and other wild creatures destined for the dinner table. At first the only other route ran south along 140th Avenue between NE 24th and Main. It turned west at Main, thence to Wilburton. The 140th Avenue section was part of the Redmond-Newcastle trail traveled by men who worked in the coal mines or who took produce to sell at Newcastle. This route angled toward the east and crossed present Highway 90 at Eastgate. Homesteaders who found employment in the mines and came home weekends either rode horseback or walked the entire length of the trail. Some of the first vehicles seen on this pioneer route were wheelbarrows, for it is related that early farmers were known to fill them with produce, take them across Lake Washington by boat and push them in to Seattle, bringing home supplies in the same manner.

A description of the country in October, 1885 told of landing at the edge of the forest and finding "everything in timber except in the small clearings which are very productive in fruit and vegetables. Blackberries are wild and abundant. It is out of the question in most places to go outside the trails; the undergrowth is an impassable barrier. Fir trees are 200 to 300 feet high, some up to 12 feet in diameter."

Ten years later (1895) three more east-west dirt roads existed, one along Main Street to Larsen Lake, another from Mercer (Slough) Landing to Robinson Landing on Lake Sammamish, a third out NE 8th to 148th Avenue, also a short piece east from Newport Landing and a side road reaching Phantom Lake. All were in poor condition. It was customary to repair the wet or muddy stretches with corduroy, logs laid together crosswise.

The Shiach Brothers

More families continued to arrive in Bellevue, among them William Shiach, logger, in 1885, and his brother, David James Shiach, in 1889. Will's property was near the corner of NE 24th and 140th Avenue NE. It was part of a Northern Pacific land grant; the Highland Community Club, now a senior center and earlier a facility for handicapped young adults, is on a piece of it.

Will Shiach was born in Ontario province in Canada in 1838 and married Kate, an Irish girl. He died in 1903 at Kirkland and Kate died in 1920. The Will Shiachs had several children. One of them was Ed Shiach

David Shiach with friends and a deer at his farm which became a veritable nature park. Photo courtesy of Marymoor Museum

who married Jessie Bechtel and another was Alice Shiach who attended Bellevue High School.

The Shiach brothers had a logging company at first. David, who lived longest, became well known in the community. In 1888 he bought the Peter Buckley homestead, 160 acres at the end of the trail running slightly southwest of Houghton. It lay between 100th and 108th Avenues NE and NE 17th and NE 24th Streets. Buckley was a carpenter and lived on the farm with his wife Martha and three children.

Shiach, originally from Kempville, Canada, went to Petaluma, California in 1874 and remained there 15 years. After making a trip north to buy the farm he returned to Petaluma in 1889 and married Rosanna Miller. They lived ten years in the old shake Buckley house before erecting a new dwelling, which they sold to Mrs. Isabel Bechtel. They constructed another on a five-acre tract, moving into it in June, 1900. The Shiachs had no children of their own but adopted a five year old girl who was sent across the lake and was to be met by one of the Shiachs. Instead, 16 year old Isaac Bechtel escorted her home in a horse and wagon. From then on they lived across the road from each other, fell in love and married in 1917. During that period one of Shiach's jobs was keeping the roads open. When he acquired an ox team he delivered large quantities of supplies to other farmers.

William Shiach's logging operation utilized corduroy roads. Photo courtesy of Marymoor Museum

Shiach, a veteran hunter, raised a herd of deer, beginning with two captured fawns. By 1910 his herd numbered 13. He kept the deer 20 years, along with other pets—foxes, a mink, raccoons, rabbits and hundreds of China pheasants—and his farm was a show place, known for its natural park. The oldest orchard in Bellevue was believed to be the one on the tract he sold Mrs. Bechtel. The trees had been set out about 1878.[11] David Shiach died in 1939 and his widow lived three years longer.

Bellevue Gets a Doctor

Dr. Charles M. Martin, who by coincidence had interned at Bellevue Hospital in New York, moved to Bellevue in 1892. He had started practicing medicine in Seattle and saw the Eastside community for the first time when he was called to attend the birth of L.P. Smith's son, Bill. Some time afterward a man selling acreage suitable for fruit growing in the Bellevue area entered his office and the doctor became interested at once, as he wished to move to the country for his health. He bought a ten-acre tract at the corner of NE 4th and 108th Avenue NE, set out apple and peach trees and built a home which stood until recent years. He was Bellevue's first physician, retiring in 1914 after 49 years of medical practice. His son Hugh was Bellevue's first mail carrier. A story is told about a night when he escorted the postmaster's daughter Emma Ivey to a show in Seattle. On the return trip they reached the lake at Leschi only to find that the last ferry had departed. Martin rented a rowboat and delivered his girl friend at home at daybreak, protesting to her father, "I can explain everything." It didn't matter, for the couple were soon married.

Land records show that two Lanier brothers, Wilfred in 1888 and Roch in 1890, bought property from the government between Northup Way and NE 8th, 156th Avenue NE and 164th Avenue NE, which took in the main Crossroads shopping district. Considerable forest still existed in that vicinity until the late 1940s. However, by the 1930s the Laniers no longer owned any part of it.

Ové Peter Larsen, a Dane, gained title in 1889 to 160 acres at Larsen Lake. He worked in the Newcastle coal mines and came home on weekends. During his absences his wife Mary frequently chased bears from the property.

Larsen was no farmer, but his sons helped to harvest potatoes and other vegetables grown at the edge of the bog. They picked wild cranber-

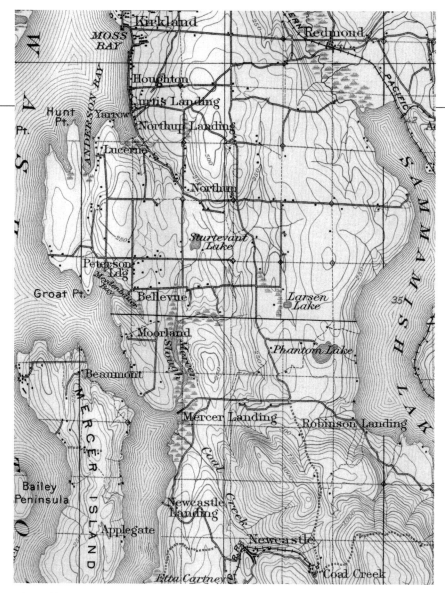

The Bellevue portion of the 1895 map published by the U.S. Geological Survey. The road between Redmond and Curtis Landing was the oldest on the Eastside and was based on an Indian trail. Newcastle was the Eastside's first population center and had a railroad as early as 1878.

ries and blue huckleberries and sold them for 50 cents a gallon in the city. The house stood where the K-Mart is now located. After the Aries brothers bought half of the property in 1913 they used the home for a cook house. Larsen felt he couldn't make a living there and, after his children were grown and moved away, he resided in Seattle, where he died in 1916.

Meydenbauer Bay in 1900. Activities on the bay included the winter headquarters of the American-Pacific Whaling Co. (1919–1942), a dance pavilion at Wildwood Park (1910–about 1930), and a Seattle-bound ferry dock (1892–1920). Museum of History and Industry, Seattle, Wa.

Maps of the 1890s indicated three boat landings on Meydenbauer Bay—Peterson's, Bellevue and Moorland. At the end of the nineteenth century Bellevue was a barely noticeable dot on the landscape, its present business center devoted to a scattering of small rural homes, fenced garden plots, cows munching long grass, chickens cackling, horses plodding along lanes or roads that were mostly a pair of ruts. It had the school near the waterfront but several years were yet to pass before Main Street achieved a grocery and feed store. A newspaper article of 1893 commented that the country was "a mine of wealth," that all it needed was finding a reasonable method of reaching market with its produce. Land values were still so low that in 1896 an acre and a half tract with a small house was taxed only $3.27.

Bellevue remained a place where men from the city went hunting, where children, after classes let out, were expected to do household or farm chores and where early mornings resounded with bird calls. The residents drew their water from wells, and kerosene lamps lighted their way to bed. Growing families saw the acres of virgin timber around them turn to stump land, then to cultivated plots. Not even a house of worship existed until a Congregational group was organized in 1896.

The First Churches

It is awful quiet around here," wrote the teenage daughter of Ové Larsen in October, 1901, "but we are going to have a surprise party at the John Sanderson's Friday night, the first we have had in over a year . . . we just stay at home except on Sunday. I go to Sunday school and prayer meeting and Jim (her brother) goes hunting and fishing."

The Congregational church was built in 1901 at the present intersection of NE 8th and 108th NE on land donated by William Raine, who three years later joined with Oliver F. Frantz in the town's first platting. They laid out lots in the central district measuring an acre and a half apiece.

Raine, a Scotsman who had farmed in Arkansas, came to Bellevue in the 1890s. Frequently when cash ran low he paid the pastor's salary. He lived in Bellevue 40 years, dying in 1931. One of his sons was the famous writer, William MacLeod Raine.[12]

The town acquired its second church, Baptist denomination, early in the present century. Corwin Shank, a Seattle attorney, looked around for a place where his father-in-law, the Rev. J.G. Baker, could live and work. He purchased a 40-acre tract in 1899 from J.B. Warren (the property was on the northwest corner of Bellevue Way and NE 8th). Shank built a large white house at the corner of NE 8th and 100th Avenue NE, and his wife's parents moved into it. Shank reserved a log cabin on the grounds as a summer retreat for his own family. The two structures shared a well, a three-hole outhouse, a barn, pig pen, chicken house and rabbitry.

Baker held his first Baptist service in the parlor of the big house, later erecting a church a few hundred feet north of the log cabin, facing 100th. The church moved again to a site now occupied by Ground Zero, a teen center, north of the Bellevue Boys' and Girls' Club.

Sam Sharpe was Bellevue's second mail carrier, employing this wagon for that purpose in 1911. Pictured is Sam Sharpe's assistant.

Corwin Shank is not to be confused with D.M. Shanks, who in 1890 purchased some of Matt Sharp's original acreage to satisfy a judgment. His land was on the north side of the present Bellevue Square Mall and in February, 1891 he laid out the Cheriton Fruit Gardens tract. Another purchaser of Matt Sharp's property was Ed Downing, who lived in Seattle but had friends in Bellevue. Shanks' realty sales included acreage to Ellis E. Powell, Hattie and Elizabeth Combs, Charles Harvey Johnson, Andrew A. Peterson, L.P. Smith, J.B. Warren and Fred Cyr.

Cyr came in 1892 with his employer, Warren, and helped the latter build a house. He worked three years at hauling cordwood for the Leschi water pumping station across the lake, then went to Alaska. After his return he raised strawberries.

Johnson and his wife arrived in 1892 and lived temporarily in the cabin that had served Jeffrey as a school. Some years earlier Johnson had been a builder, and he saw a use for the first Meydenbauer Bay schoolhouse that had just been abandoned. He bought it, dismantled the structure and soon the windows, doors and some of the lumber were components of the house he was building for himself.

In 1900 Johnson sold his place to Sam Sharpe, who later worked for the Hewitt Lea sawmill until in 1911 he became Bellevue's second mail carrier. Sharpe helped enlarge the Main Street school building and, because of the family's long residence in the community and the similarity of names, it is often assumed he was one of Bellevue's founders.

The Railroad Reaches Midlakes

Construction of the Northern Pacific Railroad in 1903–4[13] meant that trains would pass near Sturtevant Lake and it would no longer be necessary to depend entirely upon boats to bring supplies from the city. The line came from the south and connected with a line that ran to the Canadian border. The 22-mile stretch between Black River Junction, at Renton, and Woodinville started as the Lake Washington Belt Line and was intended to serve the coal mines and the steel mill planned at Kirkland during the town's boom years. The depression of the early 1890s ended that project before all the track had been laid. The Northern Pacific took it over, changing the route (once intended to follow 112th Avenue in Bellevue) so that it did not have to cross the treacherous slough where bridge pilings easily sank into the bog. Oft-repeated stories about an engine submerged there have no element of truth; the rails were never laid that far. Instead the right-of-way was relocated farther inland and this necessitated the high trestle to be seen today, now part of the Burlington Northern Route. It is at an exposed and vulnerable spot, causing the structure to require frequent repairs and partial rebuilding every ten years. It measures 984 feet in length and originally crossed 98 feet above Mercer Slough. When the cars began rolling twice daily through the flag stop at Lake

At Wilburton, where the original Lake Washington Boulevard crossed Kelsey Creek. The building on the left is the Hewett Lea sawmill hotel and dormitory, which was demolished about 1920. The railroad trestle still stands. King County Public Works

Sturtevant, G.W. Rittenhouse purchased from Sturtevant a small piece of land near the south end of that body of water and opened a store. When L.D. Godsey (who had arrived in Bellevue in 1901) bought out Rittenhouse he called the place Midlakes. He enlarged the store and sent one of his sons driving a circuit, taking grocery orders once a week and delivering them by wagon.

A blacksmith shop opened across the road a few years later and Midlakes became the commercial center of Bellevue. Its industrial center was not far distant, for a sawmill had moved in at Wilburton in 1903 after a logging camp operated there. Bull team logging ended about 1907 and donkey engines were replacing oxen in the woods. The mill was one which had been at Tokul Creek near Snoqualmie and was acquired by a newly formed company, one of its members being Wade Hewitt. A mortgage carried by Hewitt was foreclosed after a slump in the lumber market. He and Charles H. Lea took over operation of the mill and continued to run it until 1918 when the trees were mostly cleared off the surrounding country and the level of Mercer Slough was lowered so that steamboats no longer could enter it to load lumber. (It had been four feet deep at the mill dock.) The firm, by then called Hewitt Lea Lumber Co., sued King County for $135,000 damages for being deprived of means of transportation for its product. The action was dismissed in Superior Court, appealed and decided in favor of the plaintiff in 1920. Today's Highway 405 crosses the old mill pond. A grocery (owned by Patrick McGauvran) that was at Wilburton burned in 1921 and soon afterward the sawmill fittings were removed from the remaining building. Children from the Wilburton School already had been transferred to the Main Street School.

Transportation across Lake Washington to Seattle was difficult and could not be depended upon by residents of the southeast portion of Bellevue. When Helen Thode Boddy was a child she would walk from Phantom Lake to Newport Landing at the mouth of Mercer Slough and hope to flag a tugboat bound for the city. Usually it was towing logs.

Nearby Newport Shores at the turn of the century was the farm of August Havercamp, a German, who about 1881 bought parts of the old claim owned by Clarence Bagley's family since 1867, when it was among the first staked east of the lake. Bagley had presumed it was suitable for a coal mine terminus. Havercamp had no interest in coal; his fields were damaged in periods of high water, when tons of waste mineral were flushed down from the mines a couple of miles above him on Coal Creek, and he sued the company for harm done. Havercamp continued to live at Newport Shores until his death in 1927.

Ferry Service Begins

A Seattle resident wrote in 1885 that the steamers on Lake Washington were "hardly larger than a tugboat and are designed for carrying freight as well as passengers. They run regularly but stop generally where some settler waves a blanket or apron as a signal."

Before the turn of the century, the *L.T. Haas* ran an extensive route around Lake Washington that included Leschi Park, Medina, Bellevue, Clyde Beach, the Moorlands and Mercer Island. Historical Society of Seattle & King County

Small boats occasionally called at Bellevue where the route to the landing was known as St. James Road before it became Main Street. Scheduled ferry service was the outgrowth of the catch-as-catch-can method of hailing passing vessels. The first regularly scheduled stops at Bellevue are indicated on a time card published in June, 1892 for the C.C. *Calkins*, a 78-foot steamer which had been launched the previous year at Taylor's mill on the Seattle shore. The card did not list Bellevue by name; instead it mentioned the following departure times "from Meydenbauer Bay": 8:20 a.m., 11:20 a.m., 1:20 p.m. and 5:20 p.m.

The *Kirkland*, a sidewheeler, was an even earlier caller at Bellevue, but came only on specific errands. In February 1889 it began calling daily at "Houghton, Kirkland, Juanita, and at 1 p.m. only departing for Newcastle and way landings."

During the financial depression of 1892–3 the C.C. *Calkins* ceased operations and was laid up at Houghton, where she was destroyed by fire about 1898. A story is told that on a windy night in November 1892 Dr. Martin was wakened by two drenched men pounding on the door of his

Bellevue home. When he invited them in they said they had come to take the physician to East Seattle (the resort community location platted by C.C. Calkins) on Mercer Island to attend the steamer's deckhand, young John Anderson, who was desperately ill with pneumonia. The trio walked to the wharf, where a rowboat had been left, and two hours later reached the C.C. *Calkins*, which had been tied up for the night.

(Dr. Martin was later honored by King County when in 1917 it built a small vessel to service Hunts Point and named it *Dr. Martin*.)

Insofar as Bellevue was concerned, another vessel was more important in providing service to Seattle. In 1898 the 67-foot *L.T. Haas* went on the run. She was owned by Alpheus F. Haas, president of the Seattle city council, who moved from Michigan to Seattle in 1890 and became secretary-manager of the Seattle City Railway, the cable line operating on Yesler Way and Jackson Street. He opened Leschi Park in 1891 and proceeded to purchase 15 acres in Bellevue, where he built greenhouses and became one of the pioneers in growing flowers and vegetables under glass. His place between NE 2nd and 4th Streets on the east side of 108th Avenue NE was known as The Ledges. Haas employed a German florist, Peter Saal, to take charge of it.[14]

Haas' next venture was construction in 1897 of the vessel which he named for his son, Louis. Operating out of Leschi as the Interlaken Steamship Co., the line was designed to make stops at Medina, Bellevue, Peter's Landing (this was evidently Adolph Peterson's landing[15] at the foot of 92nd Avenue, later called Clyde Landing), Moorland (south of Burrows' property) and Mercer Island.

Haas' era of steamboat prosperity did not last as long as he had anticipated, for times were hard. No records indicate how he happened to invest in the *Emily Keller* in 1904 when she belonged to the Bartsch and Tompkins shipyard at Houghton. Before the end of the year he sold a third interest each in both her and the *L.T. Haas* to Harry Cade and

Louis Carlson, captain and engineer respectively of the latter vessel, for the sum of one dollar apiece. The new owners had the *Emily Keller* lengthened 50 feet and gave her a new engine and boilers, also a new name. They rechristened her *Wildwood*. While this was going on, three acres of the former Meydenbauer land claim were purchased from the Kinnear estate by the boat operators and Wildwood Park came into existence at the head of Meydenbauer Bay. By 1906 Cade and Carlson were advertising excursions to the park, and when big parties were held there, they removed the dynamo from the *L.T. Haas* after the last run and used it to light the dance floor at the new waterfront resort.

Captain John L. Anderson, the former deckhand of the *C.C. Calkins*, bought the *Wildwood* when he organized his world fair excursion fleet in 1909. An oil company had libeled both of the Interlaken Steamship Company's boats for overdue fuel bills. They disappeared from the lake

The old dock at Clyde Landing on Meydenbauer Bay as it looked about 1908. This was earlier called Peterson's Landing.

Wildwood Park depended on Seattle-based day vacationers. When the ferry ended in 1920, business abruptly declined. A new owner in 1928 tried converting the pavilion to a roller skating rink, but that collapsed and the building was in ruins by 1933. In 1979 the City of Bellevue purchased two acres for a new Wildwood Park. Shown above is the Dance Pavilion at Wildwood Park.

within a few years, the *Wildwood* burning in September, 1910, a total loss, and the *L.T. Haas* being condemned in 1913. She was dismantled at Houghton, towed to the middle of the lake and set afire.

Wildwood Park Lives On

Wildwood Park survived this period and old residents remembered events staged there, Seattle groups often bringing their own bands to furnish music. Kay Neumann, later a Bellevue merchant, said the first time he saw the park was in 1912 when as a boy he attended a picnic held by the Scottish Association of Seattle "on the bay where the yacht club is now." He added, "What a day that was! They brought bagpipes, drum and bugle corps and highland dancers across on the ferry and had a high time of it."

Isaac Bechtel's daughter, Maude, recalling her childhood, said that when she was attending the Meydenbauer Bay school her mother warned her to stay away from the park, though the children sometimes slipped in there during the lunch hour. "The trouble," she explained, "was that on Mondays we might encounter a few leftover drunks who had missed the last Sunday night ferry."

Advertisements show that Anderson, after buying out all of his competitors on the lake, continued to serve Wildwood Park and it re-

Canoeing on Meydenbauer Bay at Wildwood Park. The park was a mecca for Seattle excursionists.

mained among the best known picnic places. Such excursions furnished an important share of boat revenue, as the normal passenger trade was not sufficient to support the ferries. They ceased coming directly to Bellevue in 1920, and the park from then on was patronized less by city folk and more by Eastsiders. (The Bellevue Community Club held its first annual picnic there in August, 1923.)

Wildwood Park was sold in 1928 to R.P. Allen and Jake Ewan, who improved the dance floor and every Saturday night staged dances there, with Littlefield's orchestra providing music and Ron Smith listed as "entertainer." Later boxing matches were held on the pavilion, and in a final phase it became a roller skating rink.

It had almost fallen in ruins when, in 1933, William Schupp moved the headquarters of his whaling fleet to Bellevue and bought the park for a country estate. He prepared to erect a mansion on the site of the skating rink, but the Second World War altered his plans.

In the years when John Anderson controlled the boats on Lake Washington, one of the first he employed for excursions to the Eastside was the *Fortuna*. A folder announcing her tours mentioned calls at Meydenbauer Bay, Mercer Slough, Factoria, and Newport. At this last place the regular ferry *Issaquah* landed automobile parties bound for Snoqualmie Falls, Newport being the road end for inland travel to the coal mines and the Snoqualmie Valley. Another familiar vessel was the little *Dawn*, which provided feeder service from Clyde, Calvert's and Eastland landings to Bellevue and Medina.

High School Commences

An old picture of the waterfront at Bellevue shows the building that was long a familiar sight at the west end of Main Street. The school erected in 1892 was soon outgrown, and by 1909 two more rooms were added, and high school classes commenced. Until that fall, advanced pupils had been obliged to travel on the lake boats to Seattle high schools.

Ella Peterson Stennett, who was born in a farmhouse on a five-acre tract where the Frederick & Nelson store now stands, recalled starting in the first grade in 1909, before the old building was enlarged. (Her father was Andrew A. Peterson, a Seattle tailor who moved to Bellevue in 1892.) She was one of ten students in the two years of high school available at that time in the old building. She finished in Franklin High at Seattle.

She told how the entire high school and the eighth grade shared a single room in Bellevue. The first graduating class in 1912—consisting of Frances Gordon and Norma Morgan—received their diplomas at a program in the Congregational Church.

Ella furnished other details about the school. The grounds were enclosed with a wooden fence having a turnstile in front. Behind the building were two outhouses. Water was obtained by pump from a well. A bucket stood on a shelf in the hall, with a tin dipper from which pupils could drink. They washed their hands in a sink and dried them on a roller towel. Most children brought lunches in covered lard pails.

Heavy snow fell in the winter of 1916 and lay about three feet deep on the ground, so the children were sent home. Some went to Mercer Slough to skate on the sheet of ice extending for a long distance from Lake Washington to Wilburton. Lake Sturtevant was another place where they could skate.

When M.F. Odle came to teach in Bellevue in the fall of 1918, he said that in all the schools in his district—including Phantom Lake, Highland, Wilburton, Northup, and Beaux Arts—there were only eight teachers. Sometimes when a teacher was ill, Odle had to instruct her class as well as carry on the duties of principal at Meydenbauer Bay.

The county health officer in June, 1919, made an examination of the Main Street school, found it full of flaws, and recommended that a

Our modern climate is much warmer than in pioneer days. As late as 1950, the North end of Lake Washington froze in winter. William S. Lagen Collection

Here are all the children who attended Bellevue's grade and high school when it was in the old building on Main Street in 1913–1914. The hair ribbons, long black stockings and button shoes were characteristic of that era. Lorraine Mowbray/Bellevue Historical Society

new structure be built. The old one, he said, allowed insufficient air and floor space per pupil, and the water was not fit to drink without boiling. While the State Board of Health the following November said the water was uncontaminated, the building itself was condemned. The local board purchased property nearby and erected a new building. During 1919, while construction was under way, the pupils had to be provided for. The south room of the clubhouse was used during the emergency and some other children were bused to the Phantom Lake School. They were carried back and forth in Sam Sharpe's Studebaker automobile, driven by Andy Sharpe, his son.

Francis G. Hammarstrom, who entered the first grade in the fall of 1917, remembered when the closing of the old building forced him to switch to Wilburton school part of the winter. To get there he tramped over a walkway two planks wide across the Mercer Slough swamp. His father did not trust young Sharpe's driving.

During the First World War, according to Hammarstrom, the school children made a contribution to the war effort. "We made gun patches," he said. "We cut 4-by-4 inch squares out of flannel that was donated by the mothers. The patches were for cleaning Army rifles. Another thing

The high school in 1912 had so small a student body that they occupied only one room of the building. They completed the last two years in Seattle.

we did was to bring peach pits from home. They were stored in tubs and were used to make poison gas."

By January 1, 1921, the Bellevue pupils were in their new building. It was known that the old site would have to revert to the Kinnear estate unless used for the school purposes, so renovation was carried on to bring the structure up to the required standards, and it became the high school.

On an average day after classes let out, youngsters went home, changed their clothes and helped their parents. Boys cleaned the yard and barn, cut kindling, filled the woodbox, milked cows, fed chickens and weeded vegetables. Girls did the housework. They studied in the evening by lamplight. Social events usually were limited to taffy pulls and pop corn ball parties. "We thought we were having a grand time," one man recalled.

Houses were heated with stoves and, if the sleeping quarters were cold, the children dressed near the kitchen range or some other stove. Eastside families were preoccupied with insuring the wood supply for the coming winter. In early years no restrictions were laid on cutting trees for this purpose, and the men seldom had to worry about who owned the land they were on. As an oldtimer observed, "In those days timber was all over and it was something to get rid of. It was said to be the best crop that poor land ever raised." Another living in a house on Main Street remembered. "You could hear whistles of donkey engines working in the nearby woods and the sound of the big saw at the Wilburton mill cutting into a log."

After a tree was downed it had to be sawed in stove lengths. The sticks were brought home on horse drawn drays and stored in a shed or special area in the barn.

Children of pioneers recalled the many forest fires when they were young. Sometimes Mount Rainier was not visible all summer because of the smoke that accompanied land clearing. After a tract was logged the underbrush and debris caught fire easily.

A lone telephone line reached Medina in 1907 and the first automobiles were acquired on the Eastside sometime between that year and 1909.

McGauvran's Store

Credit for opening the first real store on Main Street probably belongs to Patrick McGauvran, formerly of North Dakota, who arrived in Bellevue in 1908. His grocery and general merchandise business occupied a building on the northeast corner of 100th Avenue NE and Main, directly across the road from the school and handy to the dock. By 1911 he had a second store in Wilburton, run by his son-in-law.

Francis Hammarstrom said, "The original McGauvran's was a genuine old-fashioned place with open barrels of peanut butter and crackers and all other things that were needed in this remote area. The Masonic lodge was upstairs. One of the early clerks was Henry Stream, who some years later had his own little grocery on Main Street at about 103rd."

Hammarstrom's parents had been in Bellevue since 1907 and Francis was born here. His father did painting and wallpapering, eventually opening the first paint store where his son helped out.

The McGauvran Store known as the Bellevue Mercantile Co. was the first general store on Main Street and 100th Avenue NE. Photo courtesy of Marymoor Museum

A former resident of Clyde Hill with pleasant memories of McGauvran's is Fred Sorenson. "When I was a kid I was often there," he related. "Dad would give me a nickel or a dime to spend at McGauvran's little four-foot case where he kept penny candy. Occasionally he had bananas, but we bought our fruit mostly in Seattle, where Mother sold her butter. No fresh meat was to be had on this side of the lake until Henry Stream opened his shop after McGauvran's death in September, 1913. Stream would buy several cuts and have them sent over from Leschi."

South along the shore below Meydenbauer Bay, Beaux Arts community was commenced in 1908, its founders selecting a site on the East Channel which in 1874 was known as Johnson's wharf, a reminder of another of the little known early settlers. Events of the same period included the organizing of two granges, both in 1909. One at Highland had 32 charter members. Another at Bellevue had 46 members, with R.C. Calloway as master and Hugh W. Martin as secretary.

About this time a stock-selling scheme was hatched to provide an electric car line running between Medina and Lake Sammamish and connecting Issaquah with the ferries. It never materialized. A large sign on the proposed route was a sales pitch for land offered at $20 an acre.

Factoria came into existence in 1910 through another promotion effort, intended to convert what had been marshland into the setting for "a smokestack city." It was to be the freight terminal of a nonexistent railroad, and would have a branch line for passenger cars connecting with the ferries at Medina. This plan collapsed before the first factory (supposed to manufacture stoves) was opened. Years later, builders of modern Factoria found surveyors' stakes where 25-foot lots had been laid out more than half a century earlier by a Chicago development company.

Midlakes

Midlakes had witnessed changes with the coming of L.D. Godsey, who built his home near the corner of NE 8th and 116th Avenue NE. A small stream flowed through the property, draining Lake Sturtevant. Godsey planted an orchard and tiled the channel of the creek. His two sons were mainly in charge of the store, where a supply of catalogues aided customers in sending away for desired items not regularly carried in stock. Somewhat later N.C. Nelsen's blacksmith shop opened nearby. Nelsen's was a busy place, capable of handling up to five horses at one time.

The Godseys operated their store until after the First World War, when they sold to G. Louche and directed their own efforts into conducting a vegetable processing and shipping warehouse.

In the meantime, another business enterprise sprang up near Meydenbauer Bay, opened about 1916 by Tom Daugherty in a triangular shaped one-story building on Main Street. Daugherty, who had previously worked for McGauvran, carried groceries, feed, and general merchandise.

Midlakes was the center of an extensive farming community in 1914 with a railroad station on the Northern Pacific Railroad. Photo courtesy of Marymoor Museum

He stayed in business less than a year and went broke. In 1920 a newly formed grange, the third one in Bellevue, rented the store, its members expecting to enjoy discounts on needed supplies. (R.S. Whaley was grange master and Mrs. F.W. Winters was secretary.)

The post office remained in William Ivey's home on Main Street until it burned in 1916. Allan Sharpe said this happened on a day when men were clearing brush in order to improve the way down the steep hill to the ferry landing. Sparks from their fire settled on Ivey's home.

"We were swimming in the bay and on the way back we saw Ivey's place going up in flames," Sharpe recalled.

The postmaster, who owned five acres, immediately went about erecting a separate building on the northwest corner of Main and 102nd Avenue NE to house his business interests. He occupied a corner of the new structure, and in 1918 his nephew, Charles LeWarne, opened a hardware store in the remainder.

The grange enterprise lasted only about six months, as Main Street became a poor place to do business after the ferry stopped calling at Bellevue and all the traffic went toward Medina instead.

After the triangular building was vacated, Charles LeWarne moved his hardware company across the street in 1921, and ran it another five years, selling to Ira H. Finnell. LeWarne also had a plumbing shop in the basement. He became postmaster in 1930, and from 1937 to 1952 the family had a variety shop.

Grange members became convinced that they could still operate a feed store for farmers profitably if they were near the railroad, so young Russell Whaley took a chance, borrowed money to buy an acre at Midlakes, and the grange furnished labor to build a store. Instead of staffing it themselves, some arrangement was made whereby Whaley rented the premises to Joseph Kardong, and grange members agreed to trade there. For a time it was known as their store.

Kardong was an energetic man, who became prominent in the community. He had traveled from Minnesota to be with relatives in Seattle, and visited Bellevue about 1910, attending a basket social at Wildwood Park. He was married in Seattle and moved his family in 1916 to what he called his stump ranch off 108th Avenue NE, where he raised produce and hired out his team of horses to clear land for other farmers. Five years later he bought five acres on NE 4th (originally known as Cherry Street),[16] west of the present Puget Power building. By then he was operating the store at Midlakes, next to Whaley's garage and the blacksmith shop. Nelsen, its former owner, had moved away about 1910, and Charles Dobbin became the smithy.

The first garage in this area was started by Oscar Vollmer in 1918 near the grocery store in Medina, moving a little later to a location diagonally across from St. Thomas Church.

George Hanson and his brother, Arvid, arrived in Bellevue in 1919 and soon opened the second garage, locating it on Main Street and add-

George Hanson, garage owner, demonstrated his height, while two of his friends stood by.

ing a car dealership in 1928. Whaley had his garage from 1923 to 1935. A news item of April 1934 noted that he had installed a new type of gas tank "which will enable the customer to purchase gas by the gallon or by the $1 worth, as so many motorists prefer to buy it."

Russell Whaley was the son of Robert Whaley and Barbara Bechtel. His father, a carpenter from Denver, arrived on the Eastside in 1892, settling first at Medina, then moving to Beaux Arts, where he built a large number of houses.

Farming continued to be Bellevue's big industry, and the railroad made possible the unloading of cars full of hay, feed, sacks of cement, and other bulk merchandise on a spur track at Midlakes. Fertilizers were in heavy demand by the farmers.

"A lot of it was organic—bones, blood, and animal meal," Kardong's daughter, Mrs. Kathleen Leptich, recollected. "People used to say Midlakes reeked of the smell. The place was a melting pot for the community, a center of everything that was going on for the farmers. Father had a big loading platform on his warehouse, and a cannery representative was on hand to weigh in fruit and send it off to Seattle."

The Japanese

"In the 1920s so many Japanese farms were around that we spoke of Japanese Row 1, extending north from Lake Sturtevant, and Japanese Row 2, south along the creek at the Glendale Golf Course. Their small tracts were of great fertility. A lot of us kids worked in the fields picking berries for the Japanese. They had a cooperative warehouse half a block long beside the tracks where they packed peas and lettuce for refrigerator cars. They got up at the crack of dawn, and some worked all night."

A few of the Japanese may have arrived in Bellevue as early as 1894. They were imported to help clear and improve property, some of which they soon arranged to lease. By 1913 they were well established and had their own warehouse and packing plant at Midlakes. Eventually they grew 95 per cent of the local strawberries and quantities of other produce. Their children formed a Japanese club in the high school, and the adults built a clubhouse in 1930 and organized a Japanese language night school.

The Numoto family working on their thriving strawberry farm. The water tower is reminiscent of the days before a city water system existed. Cano Numoto

The Japanese had a special portion of the old Pioneer Memorial Cemetery, now the site of a medical building on 116th Avenue NE. When the land was sold, ceremonial dust was taken from there and reburied in two plots at Sunset Memorial Park, where the names of some of the colony's families are preserved.

The Japanese community not only operated a farmers' warehouse, it had social clubs and in the summer of 1930 the community celebrated completion of its $6,000 club house on what was known as the Dill tract near NE 10th and 102nd Avenue NE. Leading citizens of Bellevue attended the dedication ceremony one sunshiny day late in July. It was estimated 500 people attended the gathering.
Cano Numoto

New Enterprises

The oldest business directory for Bellevue was issued in 1911 and listed only two stores, probably referring to McGauvran's and Godsey's. Two years later the community had three stores. A promotion booklet went on to enumerate three grammar schools, one high school, two churches, one blacksmith shop, the Wilburton sawmill, and a shingle mill. The area, it said, consisted largely of two-to-ten acre tracts with orchards, berries, and greenhouses. Midlakes was still the commercial center, and Main Street had small farms on either side. A jitney bus connected Wilburton with the ferry dock at Medina.

The State Gazetteer and Business Directory for 1913–4 described Bellevue as follows: population 750, Congregational and Baptist churches, Pacific and Independent Telephone Co. connections, 12 daily mail boats to Seattle and these businesses: Godsey and Sons, grocers; Hewitt-Lea Lumber Co.; William T. Ivey, postmaster; Patrick McGauvran, grocer; Charles M. Martin, physician; Eugene M. Sherman, compass manufacturer; Thomas W. Sloan, physician. (Sloan had shared an office in Seattle with Martin, and at the latter's suggestion moved to Bellevue in 1912. He died in 1923.)

"About 1914," Rody Burrows recalled, "it was a big deal for me and my sister to walk to Midlakes to see the train go by. We would walk all the distance from home out NE 8th to Godsey's store and not see a soul along the way. Think what it's like now—they say that same street is one of the busiest in the entire state."

When Dwight Skinner in 1912 quit logging and bought from another logger named Churchill 40 acres to farm at the intersection of 148th Avenue NE and NE 8th Street his only neighbors were men cutting shingle bolts from downed trees. His children attended Highland School and his son remembered, "We were on the outermost limits of civiliza-

Bagging carrots at the Aries farm at Larsen Lake. Photo courtesy of Marymoor Museum

tion. The logged-over land was covered with wild blackberries. Father raised chickens, as many as 5,000 at one time."

An agricultural enterprise that was to become important to Bellevue was the truck farm started in 1913 on half of Larsen's land, purchased by Louis, Tony and Albert Aries from South Park. It consisted of 80 acres, mostly lying between Larsen Lake and Main Street. The farm was the outgrowth of a fruit stand Louis Aries operated in Seattle. The brothers raised peas, potatoes, wax beans, cauliflower, carrots and celery on a large scale and, most important of all, carloads of iceberg lettuce, some of which was shipped as far away as the Philippine Islands, Yukon Territory and Alaska. A sideline to shipping produce was the manufacturing of crates for the vegetable farms.

To backtrack again, Bellevue acquired a new industry in 1911 when Eugene Sherman opened a compass factory at NE 1st Street and 100th Avenue NE. He had been making the instruments in New England and decided that the many fishing boats on Puget Sound offered an outlet for his product, so he moved west. He started in a small building next to his home, constructing it with scrap lumber and windows salvaged from structures torn down after the World Fair in Seattle. A couple of electric motors, with belts dropping down from above, powered the machines. Sherman had a small bronze foundry to make castings. Everything had to be non magnetic except twin balls on either side of the compass and these he had cast in Seattle.

When weather was cold some of his employees worked in a room off the kitchen of his house. Much fine assembly work was involved; everything had to be precise and balanced. It required at least a day to assemble a compass; some special ones took a week. Generally Sherman employed five persons, but during the Second World War he had as many as 18. The factory ran until 1944, when it was sold and moved away.

Mrs. Alice Williams Sherman was even better known than her husband. A violinist with a charming personality, she maintained a studio in Seattle and taught music there as well as in her Bellevue home.

Telephones Come to Bellevue

While the telephone already had crossed the lake to Medina, it was December 28, 1916 before it was connected in Bellevue. The first exchange served 40 phones and in five years this number increased to 125. Emma Jensen, a former operator at Medina, said when she was hired in 1922 the job involved more than putting calls through. "I took in bills and did whatever else had to be done around the office, including recharging batteries on the switchboard. The back of the office was fixed up as an apartment where I lived. The night operator would go to sleep on a bed that was set up in the office for her."

The Reflector, Bellevue's first newspaper, offered a glimpse of the early

The ferry *Leschi* provides a backdrop for Phyllis Hill Fenwick and her friend who are enjoying the water in Meydenbauer Bay. The line from Leschi Park ended in 1920, however ferry service continued on the Seattle-Medina run. Phyllis Hill Fenwick Collection

years of this utility when the editor wrote, "Don't get peeved if the phone service is mixed up—there are so many new ones (subscribers) it is hard on central."

Not until 1948 was a new main office opened in Bellevue. The original one at Medina was closed and became the post office building The reason phone service started in the latter community was because Edward E. Webster, head of Seattle's Independent Telephone Co., erected a summer home there in 1905.

A few electric power lines were strung along country roads on the Eastside in 1902, but this service was also delayed in reaching Bellevue. Not until December 1913 could residents quit depending on lamps and

Although the automobile age had arrived, horses and buggies still met the ferry in 1914 at Bellevue's dock. MSCUA, University of Washington Libraries, 1914 (Lee 2373)

candles. Some outlying districts did not get electricity until 1927. Power lines appeared along the roads and in May, 1914 a few street lights were installed. That same year an automobile ferry, *Leschi*,[17] was placed on the Lake Washington run and work commenced on the highway through Snoqualmie Pass. The route approached nowhere near Bellevue; however the Bellevue-Redmond Road was improved.

Hertford and Southview

Medina already had a few summer homes on its lakeshore, and in 1915 several were erected at Enatai, close to where Highway 90 now crosses the East Channel. Judge Robert Brook Albertson bought 48 acres of waterfront property and encouraged relatives to build cottages there. Whole boatloads of friends were invited for picnics, among them prominent medical men, for one of the houses belonged to Dr. James Tate Mason of Virginia Mason Hospital. The colony at that time was called Hertford, for the judge's birthplace in Virginia.

A former guest recalled that ice was delivered by motorboat twice a week, and roadside stands furnished fresh vegetables. A Japanese farmer nearby sold peas for one cent a pound if visitors picked them.

A few hundred feet up from the water in an area then called Southview (110th Avenue in Enatai), Dr. A.C. Holmes, a Seattle dentist, started a ten-acre holly farm, patterned after one his friend, Edward Tremper, began on Yarrow Point. Tremper bought the Enatai farm after the dentist died and operated it 13 years. Holly still grows wild in the neighborhood.

More exotic than most of the houses erected on the Eastside by the wealthy was a European manor on some of the original Downey property on Clyde Hill. It was built by Max Freed, a Hungarian, who embellished

A group enjoying the swimming in Meydenbauer Bay when there were no limits to available beaches and fences did not bar one from private property. Burrows/ Warren Collection

Meydenbauer Bay circa 1930. William S. Lagen Collection

his garden with a fountain and statue. Fire destroyed the home in 1917 and the estate went back to nature until R.E. Rogers of Seattle built 85 homes in the area that became Vuecrest.

When the level of Lake Washington began to change in 1916–1917 with construction of the ship canal, the sawmill business at Wilburton was forced to end. This led to the closure of the school in 1919 because it cost too much to keep it open for six children.

Private docks along the lakeshore were left high and dry as the water receded. Boats could not approach the landing at Southview, and navigation in Mercer Slough was completely blocked. Although the United States Engineers Corps sent a snag boat to remove timbers where craft were prevented from approaching the wharf, residents were complaining as late as 1920, "We are in a deuce of a fix without a boat being able to land."

Fred Sorenson remembered as a boy of 15 walking around the edge of Meydenbauer Bay, and seeing freshwater clams standing on end in the sand because of the retreating water line.

By 1918 Bellevue had grown a little. St. James Road (Main Street) was recently paved. The community had a newspaper, *The Reflector*, two blacksmith shops, a post office, and on the dock a metal letter box, nine daily boat trips, nine store buildings, and a bank that was started in a small structure midway between Main and 1st Street NE on the west side of 100th. Begun in 1915 by Earl Bigelow, a realtor, the State Bank of Bellevue closed less than three years later because of too little patronage.

The Reflector

The Reflector, a three-times-a-month "magazette," made its initial appearance on January 1, 1918 and was printed on borrowed paper at a shop in Seattle where the new publisher, E. Eugene LeHuquet, had worked as a printer. (According to Sylvia LeHuquet the paper was printed in a tent for a short time.) Though his name sounded foreign, he was born in Iowa. His mother was American, his father, of French descent, was from Quebec. Besides editing the initial newspaper in Bellevue, LeHuquet operated the town's first motion picture projector and sold flavoring extracts as a sideline. He was a member of the school board and for a while its chairman. The five oldest of his nine children helped gather news, subscriptions, and advertising for the paper. His daughter said they didn't learn housework but how to set type and print. Nearly all of its first year the editorial office was in a 10-by-12 foot tent, ill lighted and overcrowded. Much of the news it published concerned the influenza epidemic and deaths caused by it.

"Nearly everybody is laid up with the flu and news is scarce as feathers on a frog," LeHuquet wrote.

When *The Reflector* moved one rainy day into its 14-by-20 foot quarters on the ground floor of the editor's new house, the printing press and accessories were brought from Seattle on an automobile truck. A block from its destination the wheels sank in mud to the hubs. Not long before that LeHuquet, commenting on the state of the roads, remarked, "If you want to learn how to cuss, try driving your car from the Overlake dock north to the Boddy dock (on the Points)."

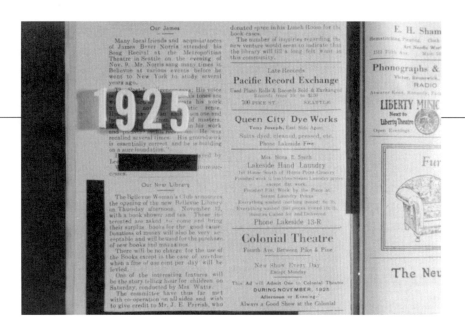

The Reflector **was smaller than tabloid size.** Bob Sandbo

Ten years after his arrival he reminisced about his impressions of Bellevue when he first saw it. High fir trees were along both sides of Meydenbauer Avenue (NE 8th Street) east of Clyde Road (92nd Avenue NE). "Main Street went into an air pocket at what is now the junction of Lincoln Avenue (Bellevue Way) and its traffic went over a bridge between the old school house and the Columbia Lumber Co. yard," the editor wrote. "In those days all the streets of Lochleven were either trails or dense undergrowth and the present paved highway, as far as Lochleven was concerned, wasn't even on any map. When a person desired to go to Kirkland from Bellevue it was necessary to go around Bellevue Avenue or Enatai Road (108th) to Meydenbauer and then over what is now North Lincoln Avenue. The road to Medina was not anywhere near as direct as it is now and nowhere near as smooth." So few automobiles were in use that it was the custom to drive horse-drawn vehicles to the Bellevue wharf and park them in an old barn before catching the boat to Leschi.

Although the newspaper was better housed, LeHuquet's press was run by foot power, he still had no linotype, and everything was hand-set. He did some job printing on the side. *The Reflector* continued to the published until 1934, by which time the children were grown and had left home, and *The American* had already been competing four years.

The Highway Arrives

Highways were inching their way into the Eastside, and in 1919 a contract was let for building a stretch between Newport and Bellevue. A sign was posted, citing the distance to Renton as 20 miles by the new route. Ten years later that figure had been cut in half.

Lake Washington Boulevard reached Bellevue from the south in June, 1920, crossing Mercer Slough on a piling bridge which was bid in at the price of $895. Both sides of the slough were risky for road building, and it is not surprising that in 1931 the trestle had to be renewed. Piledrivers, working through peat and quicksand, finally found solid bottom 95 feet below the surface.

Bellevueites celebrated completion of the highway link with Seattle by staging a community picnic in Wildwood Park. By then some of the farms lining Main Street had given way to 27 businesses, 16 of which were in brick buildings. They could not have been very impressive, for in 1922 the community was described as "mostly a crossroad with a drug store."

This was not an entirely accurate statement, for the initial pharmacy was not opened until May, 1924, when R.M. Walker, who already had a drug store in Renton, established his "number two" in Bellevue. (It later became the Lakeside Drugstore.) It was equipped with a soda fountain.

Advertisements in 1919 issues of *The Reflector* are a guide as to just who the early businessmen on Main Street were. They mention Thomas Daugherty's store, Charles LeWarne's Bellevue Hardware and Supply Co., Calloway's Cash and Carry (which had moved into McGauvran's building), and Everett Smith's barber shop and pool parlor ("Tables reserved for the fair sex."). Another tenant in the McGauvran structure was the Twins Bakery, managed by E.E. Carney, who offered a plate of ice cream with every 25 cent purchase.

A confectionery and small boathouse had been opened earlier at the ferry landing by Henry Wiggin, who depended largely on trade from Wildwood Park patrons. He expanded and began serving lunches, but by 1918 he had sold out and gone into the hauling business. The purchaser of the lunch room and confectionery was Henry Wagner. His Wildwood Lunch had a competitor in Mrs. Grace Sandell's Bellevue Lunch and Confectionery, also at the landing. It is difficult to believe that the limited space there accommodated two such similar businesses. Wagner annexed a smaller structure at the site and converted it into a pool room. He advertised, "Pay Your Light Bills Here," whereupon Mrs. Sandell invited, "Come In and Wait for the Boat."

When the ferries ceased coming to Bellevue, both lunch rooms retired from the scene. Mrs. Sandell's was razed, and the lumber was shipped by scow to Clyde Landing, to be built into a house. That same year Wagner bought a lot opposite the Sloan residence and moved the Wildwood lunch to the highway, where it became the Bellevue Inn. This was not a hotel, but served special dinners. Wagner sold it in 1928 to R.J. Orth, who had been a head waiter in New York.

By 1919, Hammarstrom had opened his paint and wallpaper store, Mrs. M.R. Cowie at Clyde Landing solicited dressmaking, as also did Mrs. J.D. Hatch. Joe Kardong was engaged in hauling, excavating, and grading, and his brother George was in concrete work.

In 1920 Sidney Bronson purchased Smith's barber shop, and not long afterward he moved it from the Ivey building to a new structure on the present Careco corner at 102nd Avenue SE and Main Street. Bronson also operated a confectionery on the same premises.

This location has an interesting feature for it closely adjoins one of Bellevue's oldest houses. Though the structure appears to be of an earlier style, it apparently was built as the farm home of Alphonse W. Philbrook, who came from Maine with his wife and two children and in 1909 bought one of the acre and a half tracts platted four years earlier by Raine and Frantz on the Meydenbauer claim. Mrs. Philbrook died in 1922, and in another 12 months her husband divided the property and sold the east half to Bronson in 1925 and the west half to G.W. Crooks, who erected a new building for a shoe store. The two merchants agreed to keep open a passage between them so that a walk provided access to the front door of the farmhouse, which became a restaurant. It is now an antique store.

The 1921 newspaper files add more names to the businesses springing up on Main Street: John Wells' and Henry Wiggin's Bellevue Transfer, Midlakes Fuel and Transfer, Henry Stream's Cash Grocery (he bought out Calloway), the grange warehouse and store, Mrs. Laura Shear's life insurance office, Dr. T.W. Sloan, and D.C. McKee's Builders Supply at the ferry dock. The Midlakes Grocery & Feed Co. had new owners.

By 1922 one could drive the entire distance around Lake Washington, though sections of the route remained rough for another decade. The

Wooden bridge in use between 1923–39 across the East Channel from Mercer Island to Enatai. (Note the hand operated draw.) Mercer Island Historical Society.

highway looped around the western edge of Bellevue, passing along Main Street, thence to 84th Avenue NE and on toward Houghton.

The East Channel Gets a Bridge

With automobile travel to Seattle made accessible, Mercer Island residents wanted to benefit from the road, so a bridge was completed in 1923, reaching across the East Channel and passing through Judge Albertson's little colony at Hertford (Enatai Park). The wooden span and its approaches totaled 1,200 feet in length. It was 20 feet wide, and in the center was 245-foot swing truss which had to be opened and closed manually. It was seldom operated, and once, when a vessel signaled to have the draw opened, the mechanism had rusted so much that it was necessary for the boat to detour around the island. The bridge was expected to take care of all the islanders' needs for the next 15 years. Actually it served two years longer, but it became so rickety that the school bus driver instructed the children to get out of the vehicle and walk across.

Completion of the bridge was the excuse for another big basket picnic in Wildwood Park. These community affairs became an annual event, guaranteed to bring out more people than on any other occasion. The picnic, sponsored by different groups, was usually scheduled for late July. It featured all kinds of races, including sack, potato, and fat men's, as well as a tug-of-war and a ladies' nail-driving contest. Prizes were given in the competition: to the largest family present, five pounds of butter; for the cracker eating and whistle contents, a year's subscription to *The Reflector*; for the worst looking car in the automobile parade, ten gallons of gas; and to the oldest married couple, a slab of bacon. The picnic dinner generally took place at 6:30 p.m. and was followed by dancing.

Clubs Are Founded

For several years community spirit had been generating in Bellevue, beginning with a District Development Club, incorporated in April 1920 with 180 members. Among its early accomplishments was the staging of a minstrel show and carnival, netting $600. For six years it managed a clubhouse, described as "a barn of a building," which had been erected in 1915 on 100th Avenue NE. It was here that Friday night movies (admission 10 cents), raffles, business meetings, school plays and dances took place. Prior to then the Congregational Church hall had been the customary scene of local gatherings, including basketball games.

After the New Year's dance in the clubhouse, ushering in January 1, 1919, it was reported by *The Reflector*, "Some of the guests did not reach home until time to do the morning chores."

A Bellevue Community Club was formed in 1929, one of its purposes being "to make living conditions clean, healthy and attractive." The two businessmen's groups merged in February 1930, but even then it was difficult to support the clubhouse. Every year $1, 000 had to be raised to cover taxes, light, water, fuel, and janitor bills.

While the men of Bellevue were concerned with securing better lake

Boys Club in 1960 was rebuilt after a wind storm had destroyed the original structure. Photo courtesy of Marymoor Museum

transportation, improving the cut-off road to Newport, advocating a new school site and more street lighting, the wives had different interests, so they founded a women's club in 1922. One of their objectives was to give children a good gathering place for dances and entertainment. Having accepted a gift of 300 used books, they opened a public library in 1925 in a long, narrow, dark room at Parrish's Café on Main Street at 100th Avenue. So primitive was it that orange crates served for book shelves.

Two years later it moved to a 14-by-24 foot building donated by John Larson. By 1931 it was changing quarters to the basement of the old school on Main Street and in 1935 it was in the southeast corner of the Boys Club House. This was thought to be the final site until growth of the town made it apparent that the library needed its own separate quarters.

Ferry Service Changes

Several changes took place on the Meydenbauer Bay waterfront. Beginning on March 15, 1921, ferry service direct to Bellevue was discontinued, and passengers drove or bused to Medina to board the vessels. A waiting room was maintained on Main Street, and in 1923 the Bellevue Transportation Co. proudly announced it was putting a new "limousine bus" on the run to Medina.

By running no farther than Medina, the ferry schedule was speeded considerably, but at first Bellevue residents were angered by the change. However, a former captain of the line pointed out, "You can't run a ferry parallel to a road. A good many people thought they could drink an extra cup of coffee in the morning, knowing they could race to Medina and catch the boat."

For a short period in 1925, Eugene Sherman, the compass manufacturer, offered some competition by operating a launch service between Bellevue and Leschi. Captain John L. Anderson, who by then had taken a lease on the county ferries, complained that Sherman was getting the cream of the morning and evening trade. The latter replied that he was in business to save Bellevue patrons from having to take a bus to Medina.

Whaling and Bootlegging

A little to the north of the county dock at Bellevue another wharf with a warehouse was constructed at the foot of 99th Avenue and here the fleet of the American Pacific Whaling Co. wintered. The firm's seven boats were reconditioned in preparation for the next season in Alaskan waters, where they remained during the entire summer. One April morning in 1923 the whaling schooner *Fresno* caught fire at the wharf, and some exciting moments followed while the ferry *Leschi*[18] and other craft attempted to tow the boats away from the dock. No fire fighting equipment was available in Bellevue, so the flames had to be allowed to burn themselves out.

If whaling was an odd industry to be headquartered in Bellevue,

Whaling pier in Meydenbauer Bay before the fire. William S. Lagen Collection

manufacturing whiskey was an equally singular one. The Prohibition law was in effect from 1916 to 1931 and the scattered woodlands throughout the farming community afforded good hiding places for illicit stills. Some were located as close in as NE 8th and 106th Avenue, NE 2nd and 108th Avenue and near the Glendale golf course. Indeed, the second largest still was at the Ledges, formerly the Haas greenhouse.

Dr. Raymond A. Kardong remembered one still he spied on as a boy after his parents, Mr. and Mrs. George Kardong, moved to Bellevue in 1923. Eventually officers discovered it not far from the present site of Overlake Hospital Medical Center. They chopped up all the bootlegger's equipment, as they did with others in the neighborhood. "We kids used to have fun breaking up the stills after the raids," the doctor chuckled.

Creeks

He also told of a creek that flowed through the present central business district and how he used to walk along it, looking for eggs left by wild ducks. The stream was nameless and simply was known as The Creek. It began in the vicinity of NE 24th Street and ran through marshy

Harpooner standing on the bow of the Westport in Meydenbauer Bay. Museum of History and Industry, Seattle, Wa.

Whaling fleet after the dock had burned in the 1930s. William S. Lagen Collection

land extending on both sides of Bellevue Way to within several blocks of NE 12th. The creek crossed from the west to the east side of Bellevue Way and proceeded in almost a straight line along the west side of 105th Avenue to Main Street. There it ran under a culvert at the intersection of Bellevue Way and continued to Meydenbauer Bay. It drained the run-off from the east slope of Clyde Hill and the logged area south of Shiach's farm.

Kathleen Leptich told how the creek passed through some of Joseph Kardong's acreage and created a good piece of bottomland for a flower garden. He grew roses and carnations and took them to the city to sell on Western Avenue. To go to school, Kathleen had to cross a small bridge over the creek on NE 4th between the present Puget Power building and the Safeway store. In winter the stream was a rushing torrent, but in summer it almost dried up. It was a major attraction for Bellevue boys.

When the water was high, Fred Kardong and his cousins, Ray and Ed, built a raft to ride on it, "My cousin Florence fell off one day," Mrs. Leptich related, "and Ray jumped in and rescued her."

"We kids liked making boats and sailing them on the creek," Rody Burrows recalled. "We'd have make-believe sea battles about where the Seattle First National Bank (at NE 8th and 106th NE) is located. We jammed planks in the creek near NE 8th and created a swimming hole. We had trouble getting the planks out because there was so much pressure behind them. We got reprimanded for making the swimming hole."

Dr. Kardong added more information. "Over the years," he said, "residents culverted the creek and diverted the flow slightly to suit their purpose. The last place covered was south of NE 4th. Probably the first area covered entirely was north of NE 8th, where John R. Hanson of Hanson Buick Co. did an excellent job of leveling and making it appear that a creek never existed."

Such fills put an end to fishing for trout and salmon in the stream.

Twin Valley Dairy Farm which became the site of Kelsey Creek Park. It was operated by the Duey family. Dr. Fernley Duey Collection

Francis Hammarstrom said that about 1920 or 1921 the culvert at Main Street got plugged, a lake formed behind it and the road washed out. "The creek filled with sand and was no good for fishing after that," he added.

Other fishing spots still existed inside the city limits of Bellevue. Dr. Kardong and his brother caught perch and catfish in Lake Sturtevant and one year, the physician said, he went to Kelsey Creek (then called Duey Creek) for salmon. "The stream branched on either side of a field where cows grazed. When the creek flooded, the fish found themselves marooned in a field in a foot of water. It was great sport for kids to chase

This truck was used to deliver dairy products. Dr. Fernley Duey Collection

those fish. During the depression I'm certain some of them found their way illegally into various smoke houses."

This reminded Allan Sharpe, "Those were the days when hard-up farm families literally lived in winter on salt salmon and the potatoes they grew. At the end of the spawning season the fish that died still had a use. Farmers speared them with pitchforks, tossed them out of the creek and carted them home for fertilizer."

While Kelsey Creek and its tributaries were excellent spawning streams for silver salmon, the area around present Kelsey Creek Park looked good to the W.H. Duey family for a dairy farm. In 1921 they rented some of the land that had been logged for the Wilburton mill. When the Dueys moved from Mount Vernon to Bellevue, no road reached as far as their house, only the bend of a disused logging railroad. The household goods had to be transferred to a small truck that bounced over the ties where the rails had been taken out. Duey cleared all the land, erected a large barn and started a dairy, his wife driving the delivery truck, laden with home-churned butter and bottles of milk. The family operated their dairy until 1942. The farm was called Twin Valley Farm, named for the two valleys on each side of where the barn is.

Their son, Dr. Fernley W. Duey, was Bellevue's first veterinarian, beginning his practice in 1946 in the basement of a house on NE 4th across from the old Chapel of Flowers which was under construction. Duey's practice extended over most of the Eastside, the only other veterinarian being in Kirkland. Duey remembers when his family first arrived. The water had been lowered only a few years before and the farm showed evidence of the lake. There were several railroad beds over which logs were transported to the Wilburton mill. Duey wrote, "A dam had been at Wilburton near where the trestle is now. Wilburton even had a railroad station at that time which burned down about 1923."

In 1926, farmers near Mercer Slough formed a drainage district and excavated a canal through the swamp in order to drain the land so that berries and vegetables could be raised on the rich bottom soil. Digging a ditch to drain the slough had been attempted as far back as 1920.

The Strawberry Festival

Growing strawberries had been a thriving industry in Bellevue ever since Pat Downey planted them among the stumps after the timber was cut on his hill. He had to take the berries to Houghton in order to be assured of boat transportation to the Seattle market those first years. The strawberry crates were enormous and a picker could fill only about eight in a day. Sometimes they sold for less than a dollar a crate.

Mrs. C.W. Bovee was responsible for making the fruit the motive for a long-lasting community festival. One night in 1925 she dreamed of a celebration featuring the strawberry harvest. When she told her husband, who was in the realty business, about her dream he said, "Why not?" and spread the suggestion of a fete among his friends. A committee of

Fourteenth Annual Strawberry Festival welcome by Wm. A. Stennett, President. City of Bellevue.

five men and five women was formed, $40 was subscribed and the first strawberry festival was staged in June 1925. It began modestly on the old school grounds near the harbor at the southeast corner of 100th Avenue and Main Street. The merchants cooperated by decorating their windows with displays of local farm products.

Bellevue was becoming synonymous with strawberries, shipping vast quantities of them. With the initial festival a success, another was staged the following June, at which more than 5,000 shortcakes servings were consumed, as well as quantities of strawberries and cream, hundreds of cups of coffee and glasses of milk. The whipping cream bill alone was more than $125. Visitors were entertained with musical programs and exhibits of products. By the third year of the festival, 500 cars from other areas thronged the roads and several large boats full of visitors anchored in the bay. Main Street was decorated, out-of-town entertainers were attracted and the festival lasted three days. The festival moved to larger accommodations in the Bellevue Club House and grounds, which extended down to 1st Street, at that time.[19]

It grew and grew, an association was formed to sponsor the event, queens were elected and by 1935 15,000 outsiders were reported attending. Profits from the affair were divided between the community club and the women's club. The festival continued to be staged annually until the Second World War sent the Japanese farmers away—by that time they were raising most of the fruit for the shortcake—and the opening of the first Lake Washington bridge made land too valuable for growing berries.

Another product from Bellevue was Island Belle grapes, which had an excellent market during the Prohibition period. Though the two principal growers, John J. Kelfner and A.C.J. Hennig, disposed of 10-pound baskets of them at fruit stands, purchasers frequently called at the vineyards and bought 400 to 500 pounds at a time for making wine. Kelfner started his enterprise on 108th Avenue SE in 1912 and Hennig began his on Clyde Hill in 1923. Other early growers were active, among them John J. Clarke, who was the first to install a grape juice plant, and James Loughran.

Hennig's son said his father used to employ 10 or 12 persons harvesting grapes in season, and three or four working in the warehouse where juice was processed. It was mainly a family operation, and the bottled juice was hauled around to groceries. In his biggest year 12,000 gallons were sold.

Also in Clyde Hill in the same period was the winery of Robert Borg, in a shed in his back yard at the end of NE 19th Street. He operated the Summit Winery more than five years. When his house burned he moved to Medina.

Another Clyde Hill family actively associated with Bellevue was that of Calvin L. Smith, who came from Ohio in 1890 and bought ten acres

Looking north at the intersection of 104th and Main Street in 1928. The country road became Lincoln Avenue and then modern Bellevue Way. Photo courtesy of Marymoor Museum

on the west side of the hill. His daughter, Bertha, became a teacher, and in later years was credited with bringing the Campfire Girls to the Eastside.

Growth in the Twenties

The 1920s were a period of slow but steady growth. Polk's Gazetteer and Business Directory for 1924 listed Bellevue's population as 878, and described the place as "a town on Meydenbauer Bay six and a half miles east of Pioneer Square, a banking and shipping point with four churches, telephones, railway express and 16 daily boats to Leschi Park." It listed the following businesses: Anderson Fuel Co., Arcadia Farm nursery, Bellevue Hardware and Supply Co., Bellevue Transportation Co. (stage), Benhurst Dairy, M.L. Bennett (contractor) and J.J. Black, dentist.

Mrs. Jennie Peterson opened the first beauty parlor that year in Ivey's store building. Other new enterprises were a dry goods store and R.M. Walker's pharmacy. Henry Stream enlarged his grocery and installed re-

frigerating equipment for meat, and in July a second meat market opened in the new Marr-Westre building.

"The business center grows," observed *The Reflector*. But Midlakes experienced a setback when fire that February destroyed Whaley's garage, the blacksmith shop and Kardong's Kash and Karry. Russell Whaley and his mechanic tried to extinguish the blaze but his overalls caught fire. He dashed for Sturtevant Lake and Charles Meyers ripped off his clothes and helped him. Japanese workers, summoned by the phone, saved some of Kardong's warehouse stock, and he temporarily moved into the former Godsey feed store.

Dr. Kardong remembered that most customers had charge accounts and the rack where their books were kept burned. "Some customers owed a couple hundred dollars," he said, "and finally my uncle figured a way to collect the accounts after he lost the records in the fire. He would sit down with his employees and do some guesswork as to how much they thought each one owed and then they would add maybe ten dollars to the figure and send a bill. The customers, on receiving it, rushed to argue and pay up the right amount they said they owed. They would rather pay the correct sum than be overcharged. It was a good way to collect."

**Two kids and a cow at the intersection of Bellevue Way and NE 8th in 1928.
This view is looking south.** Ditty Collection, photo courtesy of Marymoor Museum

Whaley was not discouraged by the conflagration. He bought a better lot across the track and erected a cement building for the garage. Kardong stayed temporarily in the former Godsey feed store. He bought Watkins out, but that building burned later on, Whaley said.

Main Street acquired an attractive structure in 1926 when the Catholic Church erected a brick building that is still standing east of 108th Avenue. The first Catholic services had been held in Patrick Downey's parlor about 1910, the priest coming from Kirkland and staying overnight in the family home. Bellevue was then considered too small to merit anything more than a missionary branch of Holy Family parish. When Noe Lanier heard that the Catholic community proposed to build a regular house of worship, he deeded them a lot and a little frame building went up on it. Lanier died of a heart attack shortly after making his gift.

The church was equipped with an organ, played by Edwin Lewes, an elderly rancher, who came to Bellevue around 1894. Father Nicholas Rafferty conducted infrequent services about once a month. No priest was in residence. The later brick church became the public library and after that was occupied by a chiropractic clinic. Bellevue's fourth church was a Christian Science chapel.

A map of 1927 shows five new places of business on the north side of Main Street: Younger's Candies, the Bellevue Realty Co., Speer's Café (home cooking), the Bellevue Garage and McCrea's service station. Nothing else was indicated between the lake and present Bellevue Way. Charles H. Younger, Jr. was living in Kirkland and walking every day to the Bellevue dock to work on the ferry until in 1922 he moved his family into a log cabin north of Bellevue Square. In 1925 the Youngers moved again to a house on NE 5th and 98th Avenue NE.

That was the year Mrs. Younger made taffy for a Masonic lodge bazaar and something strange happened to it. Instead of hardening, it turned creamy. She did not have time to make a second lot, so took the sweets to the bazaar and gave them away. They were flavored with mint and were an immediate hit, which convinced the Youngers it might be a bright idea to make more of them at home and sell them. Next year Younger

Bellevue's Congregational Church was the first house of worship. Congregational Church

This picture of the Sacred Heart Catholic Church on Main Street was taken in the spring of 1927. The first mass was held December 1926. The building later became a public library. It still stands near Toys 'R Us and is used for offices.
Jo Downey Burke

opened his candy shop and produced a variety of confections. Soon he was employing helpers; his brand became so well known he moved the factory out of his basement and into a building in Kirkland in 1938. Only oldtimers today remember that Bellevue once had a famous candy store.

In the years when Younger was starting his business, the northern part of Bellevue Square was devoted principally to poultry farming. By 1935 one of the largest chicken farms in King County was there. Main Street had been the principal route to the ferry dock established by the county at the foot of 100th Avenue NE, where the Meydenbauer Yacht Club now is. Traffic shifted somewhat when the ferries discontinued calls in Meydenbauer Bay, and Medina became the terminus for the entire area. NE 8th Street, then known as Meydenbauer Street, was a more direct course between Midlakes and the dock at Medina. As population and the number of automobiles increased, both streets benefited when it came to the development of shopping facilities. Unlike today's arrangement,

108th Avenue SE was the original means of entry from the south, as shown on a map of 1911. It was known as Enatai Avenue and berry farms were located where it crosses Main Street.

The Reflector in 1930 listed businesses on Main Street: the Puget Sound Power & Light Co. in the McKee building, to which the post office had also moved; the Carter barber shop and Mrs. Florence Carter's tea room,[20] the Bronson building; the bus waiting station; Lewis barber shop; J.R. Jones, William Stennett, J.A. Evans and A.J. Ownbey service stations; the Sharpe building occupied by Eminson's Bellevue Dry Goods store; the bank building; the Chain grocery; a jewelry store; dressmaking shop; several real estate companies and the Marr building. The town by then had four doctors.

The new Sloan building housed the Masonic Hall, Kardong's second store, Columbia Lumber Co. and Emil Thiem's Bellevue Plumbing Supply. These were in the third Sloan building on the site, fires in 1922 and 1923 having destroyed its predecessors.

Four merchants were now at Midlakes instead of one. They were Russell and Robert Whaley's garage, G. Lauche's Midlakes Grocery, Joe's (Kardong's) Place with the new warehouse and packing shed, and Midlakes Feed and Fuel Co. The Anderson Fuel and Transfer Co. was at Wilburton.

During the preceding decade the business community had grown from 10 to 50 firms and the population had not increased proportionately, rising only from 2,500 to 3,300.

James Ditty

James Ditty, a Seattle engraver and one of the founding group at Beaux Arts, bought his first automobile in 1924 and four years later a friend told him the county commissioners were trying to find a better and shorter route than the roundabout one existing between Bellevue and

A PLAN FOR THE EAST SIDE — AS ENVISIONED IN 1928

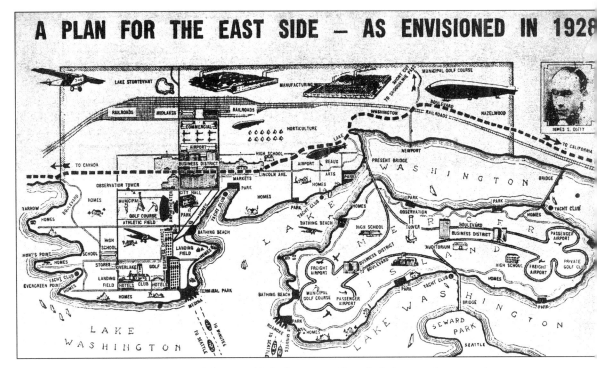

Ditty's plan for a model city published in 1928. It included more than one airport for Bellevue.

Kirkland. Lake Washington Boulevard followed 85th Avenue whereas it would be more desirable to shorten it by cutting across along present Bellevue Way, which at that time was a cow trail known as Peach Street. One of the property owners was asking an unreasonable price for the right-of-way and the friend suggested that Ditty buy the piece (opposite today's Safeway store) and acquire options on adjoining land. He followed the advice, clinching ownership of 38 acres and giving the county the right-of-way through the strip.[21] A paved street was completed in 1930 and the name was changed to Lincoln Avenue, later becoming 104th Avenue then Bellevue Way.

In the 1930s when Ditty erected the quarters for the Lakeside supermarket, the first step was taken toward creating the Bellevue Square shopping district. Ditty was a patient man, content to wait until land values increased. Taxes were low and he rented ten acres as pasture for a pair of horses. He refused to part with any for residential use. His first important land sale was to Kay Neumann for a lumber yard at NE 8th and Bellevue Way.

Ditty predicted a day would arrive when 200,000 persons would live east of Lake Washington, so he drew a plan for a model city and promoted the idea that Bellevue should incorporate. Nobody was interested and an artist friend, Sam Goff, enjoyed teasing him with cartoons about his Ditty City, which were published in a Seattle paper. Ditty didn't like being made fun of—he was dead serious about his view of the future.

Ten years were yet to pass with the central square and it surroundings mainly devoted to farming. Apple orchards, berry patches and a vineyard thrived where the mall and many of today's commercial struc-

Rubie Sharpe and her twin brothers, Andy and Tom, walk along one of Bellevue's early byways. It is near "Bonnie Brae Farm" owned by their uncle Charlie Gordon. This view today would be looking North on 108th Avenue NE and NE 8th. City of Bellevue

tures have arisen. Civic improvement were mainly lacking. For instance, there was no water system. At first water had been carried by the bucketful from wells or pumped to back porches. "We always had to be careful of the water in July," Mrs. Godsey recalled.

The next step was to bring water short distances through wooden pipes. One such system relied on a well on the Rev. Strong's property on 97th NE which was powered with a gasoline pump. Some other arrangements depended on windmills at Midlakes and Wilburton Hill.

Wells were satisfactory sources until in 1917 the lowering of Lake Washington brought the water table down, causing shortages. Patrick Downey came to the rescue because his well on Vuecrest was unaffected. An association, the Bellevue Water Co., was formed in 1923 and dug more and deeper wells, but encountered trouble[22] in keeping gravel out of the pipes. The firm erected a wooden tank in back of the present Lutheran Church (at 96th Avenue NE and NE 8th) and later a concrete one, but the population kept growing and many shoreline residents had to solve their water problems by running pipes far out into Lake Washington and using small pumps to bring water to their homes. This method sufficed for some years to come.

Highland

In the interests of socializing, a group of Highland residents in 1923 banded together and formed the Kent Corner Community Club, named for the Kent family who donated a site on the Bellevue-Redmond Road for a frame clubhouse. Members did all the land clearing and construction. Minutes of the meetings tell of the purchase of three gas lanterns and chairs at a cost of 75 cents apiece. Men brought shovels, hoes and carpenter tools from home sometimes on Sunday and worked on improvements while the women prepared and served lunch. The hall acquired a piano and oilcloth-covered tables, a well with an electric pump and finally a kitchen sink.

Besides serving for Saturday night dances, the building was used by the Sunday school. In 1926 it was wired with electricity and enlarged. The following year the group incorporated as a community club the name was changed to Highland, and the hall was rented to the grange and for private parties. It also served as the election precinct. By 1938 the community club took steps toward erecting a larger structure a few blocks away and obtained help from the Works Project Administration. The attractive log building that resulted is now a senior citizens center.

An annual Bellevue event later in the 1920s was the brief visit of participants in a lake-encircling walkathon sponsored in Seattle. This brought hundreds of hikers competing in what was facetiously referred to as the "bunion derby." As they arrived from the direction of Renton, Bellevue residents treated the competitors to refreshments before they resumed their long trek toward Kenmore and around the north end of Lake Washington back to Seattle. Some gave up at the half-way point in Bellevue and boarded the ferry to the city.

In 1930 James B. Murphy, a Seattle attorney, purchased 18 acres at Killarney on the East Channel for a Y.M.C.A. summer meeting place known as the Friendly Indian Camp. It was once visited by a real Indian chief, William Shelton. After Murphy's death, ownership was lost in 1938 and the camp moved to Orcas Island.

Depression Years

Like every other part of the United States, Bellevue had to weather the depression years of the early 1930s and little public spending was done. Young people felt the pinch when support for high school baseball was curtailed and funds were lacking for a high school annual. Employment

Looking north from Highway I-90, showing the farms still in South Bellevue. Bellevue Way and Mercer Slough are in the foreground. Robert S. Betts

was spread thin and much food was raised at home. One benefit, however, was the improvement of roads and construction of a new Highland School with W.P.A. funds.

A new type of planting was the five-acre blueberry field W.B. Sydnor set out with 7,000 plants in the vicinity of the present John Danz Theatre. At times he had 30 to 40 pickers at work. He did some canning of blueberries and sent shipments east.

Bogs were more adaptable for growing these berries, and later others planted them at Larsen Lake and along the western border of Mercer Slough. Best known in recent years was the Overlake farm, set out in 1947 by Mr. and Mrs. Earnest Van Tine. The longest surviving agriculturist on the bog bordering the slough was the late Andrew Balatico, a Filipino who began raising vegetables there in 1935.

Blueberries gained as much importance in Bellevue as strawberries had in earlier years, and for a while blueberry pie succeeded strawberry shortcake as a symbol at festivals, being regularly featured at the annual arts and crafts fair.

The Mercer Slough bog was said to be the deepest one in Washington. Mrs. Van Tine recalled, "Down Qualheim Road[23] south of our bog was an old railroad company fill where the line was to have crossed the slough, but the place wasn't suitable. They also tried to cross 112th Avenue and gave up. We saw two patches of the old pilings in the slough."

Floral products were grown around Bellevue and shipped from here. A Kent bulb grower, Fred Delkins, maintained a warehouse accessible to the tracks at Midlakes and once shipped from there to New York an entire carload of narcissus and iris bulbs.

Kinley blueberry bog near Mercer Slough with the Balatico farms in the foreground. Harriet N. Watters

Community Problems Arise

Community problems again arose in the fall of 1931, and C.W. Bovee focused attention on the need to incorporate in order to provide a better water supply and some sort of fire protection so as to reduce insurance rates. "We have the unusual distinction of the sloppiest looking Main Street on the Eastside," he insisted.

The storm of October 21, 1934 did not help the situation, for it strewed fallen branches and wires over roads and damaged buildings. One end of the big barn at Duey's dairy farm was crashed in and a porch was lifted off a judge's residence. The roof of the Bellevue clubhouse was another casualty and many chicken houses, garages, and fences were blown down. When officers of the Community Club viewed their building after the high wind they decided to remove what was left of the structure, raise funds and construct a new one.

A flurry of activity followed. Main Street was repaired in the fall of 1935 and 120 barrels of oil were spread on it "so carefully it was believed the surface would last a lifetime." The businessmen thanked the county commissioners for the improvement, saying they had labored many years to secure it. The public library, sponsored by the women's club, moved into the new clubhouse, and Mrs. Marguerite Groves became the first paid librarian after the library became a part of the King County Library System in 1944.

Another achievement of the mid-1930s was the improvement of the Bellevue school building and laying out of a football field by the W.P.A. The Bellevue Water Co. decided to construct two 100,000 gallon tanks to replace the 40,000 gallon one. Both the old and new were on Downey Hill.

Meta Burrows

A feature at the corner of 102nd and Main Street was the Lakeside

Drug Store, which Meta Jacobson Burrows took over from Charles Mayrand in 1934. (He had bought it from Walker in 1929.) Her father acquired the business for his daughter after she graduated from pharmacy school. Meta married Don Burrows, who had a butcher shop. She was the pioneer of women in management in Bellevue. A charter member of the Chamber of Commerce, she attended the early sessions of the Business Men's Association meeting in Midlakes around the pot-bellied stove at Bill Little's[24] feed store, which kept open evenings. The store would hold only about a dozen persons, but this did not matter as the group was a small one.

Meta's soda fountain was another gathering spot where many community projects germinated over coffee and cinnamon rolls. Her store was originally the bank building, and when she held the state liquor license for Bellevue from 1936 to 1942 the teller's cage served as the liquor store.

When Meta closed her pharmacy in 1979, hers was Bellevue's oldest continuously operating business.

Another commercial establishment in the early 1930s was the garage which William A. Stennett, an automobile mechanic, opened at the corner of Main and 104th Avenue (the present Jack in the Box location). Stennett was married to Ella Peterson. He had previously been employed by George Hanson.

In 1936 Cameron (Kay) Neumann purchased a piece of apple orchard at the northwest corner of Bellevue Way and NE 8th from Jim Ditty and opened a small store carrying building materials.

"I thought this was a logical location if we ever got a bridge across the lake," he explained. "This was a natural crossroad. Early in the morning and late in the day a substantial amount of traffic went by on the way to and from the ferry. The north and south traffic was modest, but if you wanted to go to Renton you went past here on what was then known as Lincoln Avenue. (Jim Ditty gave it that name.)"

Intersection of Main Street and present Bellevue Way when the Stennett Service Station was on the southeast corner.

On many days Neumann saw only two or three customers. Much of his turnover was in wood for repairing fences and farm sheds. Bellevue had no architects, it had no town government, no police except travel-ing deputy sheriffs furnished by the county.[25] It had no fire department and in April, 1935, when the whaling company had a second fire that destroyed its dock and machine shop, firefighters came clear from Kirkland and joined 50 neighbors in battling the blaze. That was the same year forest fires were fought by C.C.C. (Civilian Conservation Corps) boys north of Factoria and toward Lake Sammamish.

The Bellevue District Business Men's Association formed in 1919, was the forerunner of other civic organizations. The Bellevue Commer-cial Club made its debut that following year and next came the Bellevue District Development Club and the Community Club. The last two in 1930 joined forces and in 1947 evolved into the Bellevue Chamber of

Commerce. At last Bellevue had an organization strong enough to achieve some progress.

Its first president was Victor Lysell, who had lived in Bellevue since 1916, when he acquired an acre of land on the west side of Lincoln Way in the vicinity of the present Bellevue High School. He participated in many public activities, was with the county road-building department, served 12 years on the school board and campaigned for construction of the first Lake Washington bridge. He died in 1963. Another prominent citizen, Robert McCormick, was active in many civic projects and also held office in city administration. It is in his honor that one of the city's parks has been named.

Enter Miller Freeman

A bridge reaching across Lake Washington was being advocated by Mercer Island residents and was strongly opposed by some Seattle groups. The impact of such a structure was realized by relatively few persons on the Eastside. The exceptions were James Ditty and Miller Freeman, owner of a Seattle publishing house and a string of nationally circulated industrial journals. He nearly missed becoming associated with Bellevue's growth. Having a yen for a country home, he bought property near Kenmore that is now St. Edward's State Park. In the summer of 1927 he was boating near Bellevue and took a fancy to Groat Point as a better site on which to build. It had been homesteaded in 1875 by Albert King and his brother, who lived in a two-room shack lined inside with newspapers. The point was planted to an orchard and about 1890 was platted in small lots and sold to Eastern investors. "By 1913 people were dreaming about a day when, after opening of the Panama Canal, Seattle would have a population of a million," Freeman's son said. "They thought the city would extend across the lake. That dream was still lingering when my father built his house."

Freeman found several owners were reluctant to sell him their lots until they saw he already owned the surrounding property. He had parted with his St. Edwards tract and was setting about erecting a mansion facing Meydenbauer Bay.

Freeman had an interesting career. His family were Virginians and his great grandfather was secretary to President Thomas Jefferson. Miller Freeman, after working as a boy on his father's newspaper in Yakima, started a farm paper of his own in Spokane, sold it and in 1902 began publishing the Pacific Fisherman in Seattle, adding Pacific Motorboat in 1908. He expanded further until he had a whole string of industrial journals.

As a Navy captain during the First World War he was instrumental in establishing a naval training station on the University of Washington campus. Though involved in civic affairs he still desired a home in the country. A friend predicted that if he moved across the lake, within five years he would be involved in more civic projects than ever, including construction of a lake bridge. The prophecy came true.

The Elizabethan style mansion on Groat Point was completed in 1928 and was one of the most striking homes on the entire lakeshore. It had 14 rooms, exterior walls of double tile brick veneer, a tile roof, and its architect designed it "to last 1,000 years." Freeman lived in it until 1951 when he sold it to Severt W. Thurston, head of the Western hotel chain. The dwelling with its landscaped acres became a tax burden and it was demolished 30 years later.

Freeman retired because of poor health, but stayed on in Bellevue until his death in 1955 at age 80 in his last home on Vuecrest. Both he and Kemper Freeman, one of his three sons, played important roles in the development of the Eastside.

Miller Freeman became one of the moving figures in the campaign that was shaping up to select a route for a span crossing the lake. Applications for a bridge were filed as far back as 1926 when several localities

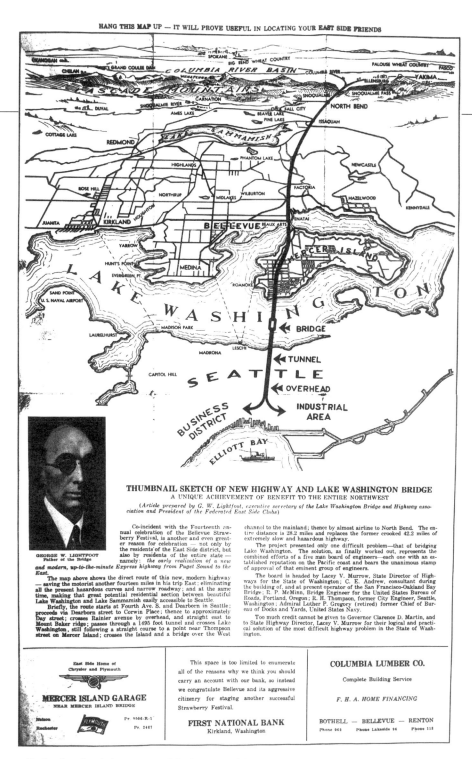

THUMBNAIL SKETCH OF NEW HIGHWAY AND LAKE WASHINGTON BRIDGE
A UNIQUE ACHIEVEMENT OF BENEFIT TO THE ENTIRE NORTHWEST

(Article prepared by G. W. Lightfoot, executive secretary of the Lake Washington Bridge and Highway association and President of the Federated East Side Clubs)

GEORGE W. LIGHTFOOT
Father of the Bridge

Co-incident with the Fourteenth annual celebration of the Bellevue Strawberry Festival, is another and even greater reason for celebration — not only by the residents of the East Side district, but also by residents of the entire state — namely: *the early realization of a new and modern, up-to-the-minute Express highway from Puget Sound to the East.*

The map above shows the direct route of this new, modern highway — saving the motorist another fourteen miles in his trip East; eliminating all the present hazardous curves and narrow roadway; and at the same time, making that great potential residential section between beautiful Lake Washington and Lake Sammamish easily accessible to Seattle.

Briefly, the route starts at Fourth Ave. S. and Dearborn in Seattle; proceeds via Dearborn street to Corwin Place; thence to approximately Day street; crosses Rainier avenue by overhead, and straight east to Mount Baker ridge; passes through a 1495 foot tunnel and crosses Lake Washington, still following a straight course to a point near Thompson street on Mercer Island; crosses the Island and a bridge over the West

channel to the mainland; thence by almost airline to North Bend. The entire distance is 28.2 miles and replaces the former crooked 42.2 miles of extremely slow and hazardous highway.

The project presented only one difficult problem—that of bridging Lake Washington. The solution, as finally worked out, represents the combined efforts of a five man board of engineers—each one with an established reputation on the Pacific coast and bears the unanimous stamp of approval of that eminent group of engineers.

The board is headed by Lacey V. Murrow, State Director of Highways for the State of Washington; C. E. Andrew, consultant during the building of, and at present operator of the San Francisco-Oakland Bay Bridge; R. P. McMinn, Bridge Engineer for the United States Bureau of Roads, Portland, Oregon; R. H. Thompson, former City Engineer, Seattle, Washington; Admiral Luther P. Gregory (retired) former Chief of Bureau of Docks and Yards, United States Navy.

Too much credit cannot be given to Governor Clarence D. Martin, and to State Highway Director, Lacey V. Murrow for their logical and practical solution of the most difficult highway problem in the State of Washington.

Early sketch of the proposed highway and bridge linking the Eastside with Seattle and areas eastward. City of Bellevue

were mentioned, from Madison Park to Juanita Point, to Evergreen Point, and from Leschi to Mercer Island, but the proposal most strongly advocated was a suspension bridge from Seward Park to the south end of Mercer Island. Freeman's help was solicited because he was known to be influential and respected in government circles. It was agreed to appoint him official spokesman for the county and in that capacity he called upon newly-elected Governor Clarence D. Martin.

Kemper Freeman, Sr. related, "Father proposed to the governor that it was time to complete the Snoqualmie Pass Highway, which then came out at North Bend and tied onto old wagon roads that wound in all directions. Father thought it ought to be laid out direct to tidewater. The governor sent him to the new highway director, who asked where Father believed the route ought to go. Father pulled a highway map from his pocket, laid a ruler down on it and drew a line over the shortest route to Elliot Bay."

Although the director at first thought such a course impossible, the finished highway does not deviate more than a third of a mile from the line Freeman indicated. As a result it passes through the southern portion of Bellevue.

Freeman foresaw the need for another road and insisted that an overpass be erected east of town for the crossing of a future north-south highway. It stood there unused for years before becoming a part of Interstate 405.

Bridges to Seattle

Ground breaking for the East Channel highway span began at Enatai with a ceremony attended by 500 persons on January 1, 1939, followed by a banquet at the Bellevue clubhouse. By April construction of the first four-lane surfaced road in Western Washington was underway, with the

A real estate advertisement expounding the ease of living in Bellevue after the Lake Washington Bridge was built.
City of Bellevue

Lakeside Gravel Co. furnishing the material.

The completed Lacey Murrow Bridge,[26] supported on cement pontoons reaching from Mercer Island to Seattle, opened July 4, 1940. Many persons expected the bridge to sink and others believed that its heavy patronage from the first day (12,000 vehicles after the opening ceremony) was due to its novelty. The opening occurred at a time when the nation was about to enter the Second World War and the shipyard at Houghton was expanding. Many families, newly arrived on the Eastside, required housing, with the result that summer homes along the shore filled with full-time occupants. The whaling dock on Meydenbauer Bay took on a new look when the facilities were appropriated for a Coast Guard repair base. The whaling guns were removed from the boats and the vessels became part of the government fleet.

Encouraged by the influx of newcomers, Kay Neumann opened the Lakeside Center in September and provided an asphalt-paved parking area for shoppers calling at his lumber and hardware store or the nearby supermarket on Ditty's land. The local newspaper hailed the parking lot as the largest in King County—its seven acres had previously been devoted to grazing livestock.

Neumann's building also housed Bellevue's first bowling alley, a bottle club and later a restaurant, drug store and optical company.

With the opening of the bridge the entire economic situation altered because of the enormous volume of traffic crossing to the Eastside. Bus service to Seattle commenced, with Overlake Transit making 26 trips

The third version of the East Channel Bridge is an essential part of the I-90 corridor. This view looks toward Mercer Island, with Seattle in the far distance. The Newport Yacht Basin is at the lower right. Harriet N. Watters

The parade celebrating the toll removal from the Mercer Island Bridge. Phil Shank and friends are in the first car not having to pay. Bill Brant, Phil Shank Collection

daily from Bellevue. Ferries ceased to run except one carrying shipyard workers to Houghton. By 1984 there were thousands of "reverse" commuters from Seattle to Bellevue.

The War Years

The impact of the Second World War was being felt by late 1941 in another direction. The 55 Japanese farmers and their families (about 300 persons in all) were shipped away to concentration camps, although many Eastsiders sincerely regretted their departure. They had been important to the farm economy, but close-in land was beginning to be too valuable for agriculture. Another indication of the war in progress was the aircraft observation tower rising high above Vuecrest. Bellevue volunteers staffed it, keeping 24-hour watch for enemy raiders. Mr. and Mrs. Grover Naslund[27] directed the work, aided by about 150 helpers. Metal scrap piles appeared at the schools and Army trucks collected the donated material. Residents learned to face the war emergency and lecturers offered advice about home defense, evacuation plans and what to do in case of gas warfare. The pinch of rationing was felt, both for obtaining gasoline and certain foodstuffs.

Birth of The Square

By the time peace was declared in August of 1945, Kemper Free-man was thinking seriously about ways to bring more shopping facilities to Bellevue to accommodate the many persons who had moved in. He had gained wartime experience in planning for the increased population shipyards brought to Vancouver. Now he consulted Joshua Vogel, a professional King County planner, who had been living near Beaux Arts since 1918.

The beloved madrona tree in front of the Crabapple Restaurant in Bellevue Square was decked with lights at Christmas time. City of Bellevue

Many people fondly remember the Bellevue Square carousel in the 1950s. Oren Barker, Pat Sandbo Collection

"We measured all of the stores east of Lake Washington," Freeman recalled, "and found out what was missing. Vogel showed me how to compute what was needed. He had a booklet that listed the towns, stores, square feet and dollars spent for them. By looking at it, if you found a community with a shortage of grocery stores you knew what more should be spent for them."

"In 1944 my father and I started buying property. At first I was going to put the new stores on NE 1st so that I'd be adding them to the same area as Main Street. I bought this property in January, 1945. I couldn't build on it in wartime so I had an opportunity to do some figuring. I asked myself if there was an advantage in having stores in a cluster. There were no books, no articles nor any association on shopping centers that I could consult. I toured the country and called on every owner of a shopping center I could find—22 in all—and asked what each had learned that was good and what was wrong."

Freeman bought ten acres from Ditty and a number of tracts in the old Cheriton Garden's plat, mostly from members of the Burrows family, who by this time had a large home where Nordstrom's now stands. The

Handicrafters could be seen at work in the Arts and Crafts Festival. Among them were some of the region's most skilled artisans. Pacific Northwest Arts and Crafts Association

first enterprise to open on Freeman's property was the Bel-Vue Theatre on March 10, 1946. Freeman had regarded building a theatre a means of encouraging some of the wartime population to remain in the community-they needed a place of entertainment. He experienced great difficulty in obtaining building materials during wartime. When the structure was completed he leased it to Pete Higgins, who had the Gateway Theatre in Kirkland. These were then the only two theatres on the Eastside. Two years later a community theatre was begun in what was known as the Surrey Play Barn. The Bel-Vue movie house operated until September, 1981.

After the movie house opened, the Kandy Kane and the Crabapple Restaurant followed in quick succession. The Kandy Kane, an ice cream-coffee shop owned by Carol Barber, was the meeting place of the local businessmen. Bruce Watson of the City Hall remembers, "Men gathered for coffee every morning and in a few minutes you could find out all that was happening in Bellevue." The Crabapple Restaurant was owned by Carl Pefley, who had been manager of the Seattle Press Club. He borrowed some local art to decorate the walls inside the dining room and observed so much interest in the pictures that in July, 1947, he arranged for an outdoor showing under the huge madrona tree that formerly stood in front of the place. People seemed delighted to purchase local art at reasonable prices and next year Pefley expanded the display with the help of a committee, including Kemper Freeman and Marjorie Hansen. The first year there were 200 participants. It was so successful that it was repeated each summer and in 1956 became the Pacific Northwest Arts and Crafts Fair, one of the largest in the United States and drawing participants from great distances.

Right in the wake of the theatre and restaurant came an early version of the Frederick & Nelson store. Freeman had induced Hector Escobosa of the Seattle department store to establish a branch as an ex-

In the early years of the Arts and Crafts Festival the arrangement of booths showed considerable originality. Pacific Northwest Arts and Crafts Association

periment in merchandising. It was agreed that if Freeman would erect a one-story building in the center of the future square, the company would rent it for three years and sell women's wear and children's clothing only. The establishment opened in August, 1946 in great style, with floodlights, searchlights, and orchestra and a radio broadcast. A demand immediately developed for other wares and the company prepared to acquire larger quarters, erecting the first unit of its present building in the mall. "It was Marshall Field's first suburban store in the entire United States," said Freeman. "For that matter, Bellevue Square was the first suburban shopping center anywhere around."

He told another story about his venture. "The only bank we had was a branch of the First National of Kirkland. When I went to the manager (I borrowed everything I could get to build the first Frederick & Nelson store) he bawled me out, said I was putting the square in the wrong place and wouldn't get any financing from his institution. He was right; the Kirkland bank only loaned to its friends and never for more than six years."[28]

"I explained to my father about the encounter with the manager and he asked what it took to start a bank. I told him and he got eight prominent fellows to go in with him and organize the First National Bank of Bellevue. It opened in a small store in a 20-by-40 foot space. The minute a competitive bank appeared, conditions took another turn and the Kirkland bank loosened up concerning the matter of loans. About ten years later Father sold to the Pacific National Bank and we built them a new building."

The Food Center (claimed at the time to be the largest food store north of San Francisco) was ready for business later in August and other construction was under way.

Dorothy Brant wrote in the March 1947 *Seattle Times*: "Frederick & Nelson of Bellevue, opened last August, is expanding this spring. The town square already includes a Firestone store, the restaurant, the Bel-Vue Theatre, a barber shop, a music bazaar, a stationery and gift store, also an Overlake Service League exchange shop."

She mentioned a large furniture store on Main Street and markets and feed stores scattered along the highway, adding that Kay Neumann expected soon to have "entire houses for sale." A firehouse had been built and a fire truck acquired and "A surge of life in the community" was being felt. She could also have mentioned that Kemper Freeman had started a radio station, KFKF.

Other Downtown Development

The writer concluded her page-long list of accomplishments with this line: "No matter how sophisticated or how built-up Bellevue may become, its general population want it to stay as folksy in thought as the auctions in the old Highland Clubhouse, as the buy-or-sell blackboard in front of the feed store, as country-like as Kay's on a Saturday afternoon, as informal as Main Street."

But things did not remain that way very long. Other developments took place in the next decade. "The Overlake School District was formed in 1942, including Medina and Beaux Arts," one resident explained. "Bellevue was then considered a nothing, being not yet an incorporated town, so that is why the district was called Overlake." The community did have a brand new $152,000 brick grade school of 12 rooms, provided through federal and state financing.

Another newspaper had appeared on the scene; in 1930 O.S. Soots and D.G. Smith began publishing *The American* in the basement of Meta Burrows' pharmacy, although *The Reflector* continued through 1934. Soon after his paper appeared, Soots suggested that the Bellevue Business Men's Association ought to become a Chamber of Commerce. He also proposed

When the schoolhouse on Main Street served as city hall, the police department was in the basement. City of Bellevue

incorporation of the city as a means of meeting some bills. He thought incorporation would more than offset the expense but apparently the citizens were not yet ready for such a move.

The publisher of Kirkland's *Eastside Journal* observed that Soots chose to issue his sheet on exactly the same day of the week, Thursday, as the one in the rival town appeared. Soots did not remain long on the scene; in August, 1935 he sold *The American* to Al Whitney. "I paid $10 a month rent and worked 16-hour days," Whitney recalled.

When the Second World War ended, the Meydenbauer Bay Yacht Club was founded. William Schupp, head of the whaling company, had become owner of Wildwood Park in 1933 and made plans to convert it into the grounds for a luxurious home. Now that whaling had ceased his son-in-law, Marc A. Lagen, interested a group of prosperous and influential men in purchasing the site for a clubhouse, which took the place of the old dance pavilion on the waterfront. The latter had fallen into disuse and was littered with rubbish. The back part of Wildwood Park was later sold to Dr. Clein and was bought from his estate by the city.

The time had arrived for Bellevue's new newspaper to come out of its basement quarter. Kemper Freeman said, "That was something my father did to help the town's growth. Bellevue needed publicity; it had no advertising medium. Whitney and his wife were getting out *The American*. I suggested to him that we could use a free shopping edition. Whitney said that was impossible. Well, Father solved it around 1946–7 by buying a 75 percent interest in the paper and hiring Whitney to run it. Father bought a new press and I furnished a better business location on the square and we saw that the shopping edition went to every resident between here and the Cascade Mountains."[29]

Rural Mail Routes

Three rural mail routes existed in 1943, the postmen using their own cars. Country roads were still bad and in winter the carriers had to be prepared to dig the automobiles out of muddy ruts or chop their way through downed trees.

Donald A. Wilson told what it was like when he was assigned the entire route south of Main Street, 35 miles in all. After calling along Meydenbauer Bay, he followed Lake Washington Boulevard to the old wooden bridge across Mercer Slough and on to Mrs. Lolita Havercamp's farm at Newport Shores. The farm, which the family occupied 58 years, was converted into the Mercer Inlet Air Field in 1946 and closed in the 1960s.[30]

"From the mouth of Coal Creek," Wilson continued, "I went up Richards Road to Grindle Hill. Grindle was an ex-logger, and old-timer who lived into his 90s. He and his brother, Lewis, bought 40 acres in 1906 at a tax-title sale, paying $500 for it. He packed in his supplies from

The new mail truck acquired in 1941. Vern Nixon, the postmaster, is seen at the wheel, with Assistant Postmaster Adelaide Belote admiring this improvement to the delivery system.

the landing at Newport, a mile and a half distant. He farmed and cut shakes for a living."

"From his place I went up the south side of Phantom Lake, where there were a few farms, and on down to Lake Sammamish and then two miles north. Quite a number of families lived along the shore, but none were above the road."

"I turned again and went along the north side of Phantom Lake. The final stretch was under the high railroad trestle and back to the post office, then located on Main Street. My sister lived near Phantom Lake, so I regularly had a hot lunch at her house."

After a storm in November, 1946, the Lake Sammamish section of the route became impassable. A rural carrier had to be a traveling post office, carrying stamps, postcards, and money order applications. In bad weather he was sometimes asked to deliver bread and groceries to handicapped persons. "It was friendly and you were on your own," Wilson said.

Water Supply

In 1946 Water District 68 bought out the old Bellevue Water Co. at a time when the latter was serving 400 customers and maintained a pumping station and a well 1,200 feet deep at NE 10th and 106th Avenue NE. Three years later an earthquake altered the strata in the well, and the operation had to be shut down temporarily while it was pumped and cleared.

This was not the only trouble with the well; one had a heavy sulphur content and another tasted of iron. It was getting so that Bellevue's water either looked bad, tasted bad, or smelled bad, so it was decided the system should pump water from Lake Washington, strain and purify it. A pumping station was installed at Enatai Park in 1951, but so many new houses were going up that two years later another pumping station had to be built on the hill south of Meydenbauer Bay. It included a reservoir, filter plant and booster station, all connected with heavy duty mains. A 50,000 gallon tank on Clyde Hill helped maintain a constant water supply, Though Clyde Hill became a separate municipality, it was in the water district.

From then on, Bellevue depended mainly on the lake for drinking water until in 1964 it arranged to buy its supply from the Seattle system, with the Tolt and Cedar Rivers as sources.

The Urge to Incorporate

At the end of the 1940s, tolls were removed from the first Lake Washington bridge and a campaign to build a second span began.

Several times Bellevue citizens made an effort to incorporate, and finally such a provision was placed on the ballot in 1951. It was defeated by a vote of 92 to 72.

With the increase in population since the bridge opened, it was apparent some overall control of the community was necessary. The Bellevue Business Men's Association had been emphatic about this as early as 1942, but the movement got nowhere, although sewage lines were

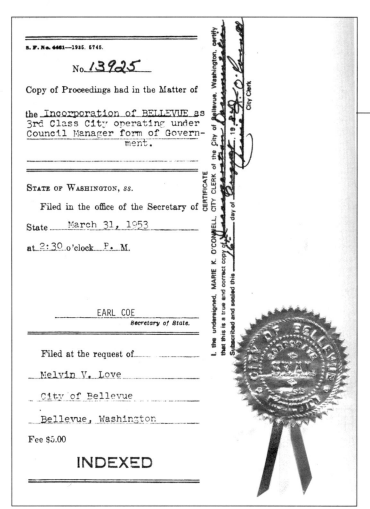

S. F. No. 4461—1935. 5745.

No. 13925

Copy of Proceedings had in the Matter of

the Incorporation of BELLEVUE as
3rd Class City operating under
Council Manager form of Government.

STATE OF WASHINGTON, ss.

Filed in the office of the Secretary of

State ____March 31, 1953____

at 2:30 o'clock P. M.

EARL COE
Secretary of State.

Filed at the request of_____

Melvin V. Love

City of Bellevue

Bellevue, Washington

Fee $5.00

INDEXED

Notarized copy of
the incorporation
document of the
City of Bellevue.
Marie K. O'Connell,
City of Bellevue

needed and water supplies were no longer sufficient. As Lake Washington became more polluted, chemicals had to be added to make it safe for
drinking. Besides these considerations, the community had always lacked
some sort of governing board; since its founding the only public organization had been the school board.

After the local clubs were absorbed into the new Bellevue Chamber of Commerce in 1947, it felt the time was ripe to unify the activities
the different groups had carried on. The move for incorporation reached
a peak in 1952 when Sam Boddy was president of the Chamber. In September a public meeting was called in the elementary school, with the
request that several representatives from each neighborhood attend and
discuss the future of local government. It was pointed out that the area

had outgrown the county level of administration, and there was a lack of coordination between existing agencies.

Following the meeting, the Bureau of Governmental Research at the University of Washington was requested to make a comprehensive survey of Bellevue and offer recommendations. When the study was completed it was proposed that a third-class city be incorporated. An election would have to be held to decide whether this should be done. The announcement stated, "It was foreseen that Bellevue's growth would be unabated, so controls are needed to prevent a way of life from deteriorating."

Voting took place on March 24, 1953, the ballots favoring incorporation of a council-city manager form of government. It was at this time that some areas, such as Clyde Hill, withdrew from the project. (Clyde Hill was incorporated separately almost immediately. One of the factors in severance from Bellevue was the fear that the size of private lots would be reduced.)

A few areas of unincorporated King County remain, such as Factoria and several blocks sandwiched between SE 30th Street on the north, 108th Avenue SE on the east and the Lake Washington shoreline. Certain residents previously had clashed with the proponents of incorporation, believing it would increase taxes. No one wished to provoke a controversy, so boundaries of the city were drawn to exclude those who did not want to be in it. As a result occupants of 26 homes depend on the sheriff's office for policing.

Four nights after the election the seven members of Bellevue's new city council gathered at the home of C.W. Bovee, the first mayor, to discuss what to do. First they had to find a place to meet. Twice they got together at Bovee's, then settled on Wednesday night sessions at the Bellevue Clubhouse.

City Attorney Kenneth A. Cole told the members it was time to discuss sources of revenue, adopt a traffic code and issue franchises for taxis, garbage service, sewer and water districts. They must also find a permanent headquarters for the town government.

Attention was directed toward the old schoolhouse on Meydenbauer Bay, no longer used for that purpose. It had been purchased from the school district by the Veterans of Foreign Wars, who offered it rent free to the city, charging only for water, lights and heat. This was a blessing, for the infant municipality as yet had no means of paying for any necessities. The proposition was eagerly accepted and the schoolhouse served as the seat of government until 1960. A bank loaned $500 in order to cover the initial expenses. The city did not even own a chair to sit on. The councilmen were green in the ways of running a municipality. They were badly in need of some employees, but had no means of paying them.

One of the council's first moves was to appoint a planning commission of nine members, two of whom were architects and another was Joshua Vogel.

John "Fred" Herman, one of the architects on the board, was soon persuaded to resign from his Seattle position and become city planner. Irving Rodley was named city engineer and the two men at first comprised the entire public works department. From the beginning the commission did not look upon Bellevue's future as that of a small town. This explains why 104th Avenue (Bellevue Way) had six lanes from the start. Businesses were required to provide off-street parking and landscaping. Everything possible was done to avoid future blight areas. In the 1960s Herman's group designed the official Bellevue logo that is still in use today.

All American City

"People here were planning-conscious before they had the legal and municipal machinery to work with," Herman reminisced. "Planning was not a strange idea to them, though a lot objected to it. There were many

1984 photograph of Bellevue Public Library with the Bellevue City Hall in the background. Harriet N. Watters

hot fights over land uses. A lawyer took a swing at me at one meeting."

Bellevue soon had cause to celebrate when in 1955 it was named an All-American City by the National Municipal League and *Look* magazine. When the award arrived schools closed early, a parade was quickly organized, a banquet was staged, fireworks were set off and a ball took place in the high school auditorium.

One of the obligations assumed by the new city was maintenance of the clubhouse where the public library occupied the southeast corner. The county library system in 1944 became responsible for its operation, the Women's Club having bowed out after sponsoring it for 28 years. When the city took over after incorporation, it allotted $40 a month for the library in its first municipal budget.

The library continued to outgrow its quarters and in 1957 was transferred to a rented basement in the Washington State Bank Building. This was the year when the Friends of the Library were organized. In 1961 the city passed a bond issue and bought Sacred Heart Church for supposedly permanent quarters for the library. The latest move was in 1967 to a new building near the city hall. This building presently has inadequate space, and several plans are under consideration by the Bellevue Library Board and the city to construct a new library at another location.

The First Police Chief

Bellevue's first police chief, G.L. Plowman, appointed in 1953, worked only part-time for the city and held down a private job as a merchant patrolman. Calls were automatically transferred to his home after hours and if he was not there, a member of his family took the information. Complaints mostly had to do with traffic, though sometimes the officers had to pick up stray cows and horses. In fact, the first case on the city records concerned a missing burro. When the town gained a solitary night patrolman, the chief signaled him by turning on his front porch light. Eventually the department moved to headquarters in the basement of the V.F.W. building.

Using the historic school as a city hall (the municipality had begun paying rent for it) had disadvantages. Mice and termites abounded in the venerable structure, and any time a heated discussion was scheduled for a council session the staff worried about whether the floor would collapse under the weighty crowd in attendance. One night it was observed to have sunk slightly from the strain on the aged timbers. Another problem was the presence of bees which nested in the women's rest room. Windows fitted badly and leaked so much that during every hard rainstorm the telephone switchboard shorted out. The oil heater was defective and spewed soot. When it conked out one fall day in 1960, the city manager declared he had endured enough inconvenience. He went forth and rented quarters in a new building on 106th Avenue NE.

The year 1956 saw several notable advances. The four-story Puget Power building was erected. Frederick & Nelson moved out of the low structure in the center of the new shopping square and into a larger store. A firm that was to become its competitor appeared on the scene; Nordstrom's opened a small shoe store facing the square. J.C. Penney also was added to the businesses located there.

A City with No Parking Meters

Kemper Freeman's theory was that providing parking as close as possible to stores carrying the merchandise which the people wanted would automatically bring shoppers. Bellevue was to have no parking meters and every business must provide its own parking space. The Square emerged as an attractive group of low structures facing a pair of wide streets with a small plaza or pavilion at the west end. Freeman intended it for the arts and crafts fair and other community activities such as Christmas caroling, tree sales, charitable plant sales and a place for a reviewing stand, if needed. The Square was described as "an experiment in flexible design." It has also been called "the key to the success of the city."

From the beginning of city government, planners had been thinking of protecting residential districts and yet providing for industrial parks. They wanted to keep the two separated and see that factories were adapted to the surroundings and had buffer strips of greenery around them.

Overlake Hospital

Apartment house construction began in 1959 and the following year saw the opening of Overlake Hospital. The need for it had been recognized a long time earlier. In the years before the Lake Washington bridge was built, it was not unusual for a Bellevue resident to die of pneumonia

Overlake Memorial Hospital in the 1960s. Overlake Hospital Medical Center

Overlake Hospital Medical Center no longer is a small hospital. Overlake Hospital
Medical Center

or a ruptured appendix because there was not enough time to get him to a Seattle hospital. While the situation improved with completion of the span, another hazard existed during rush hours, when it was impossible for a car with an invalid to avoid traffic jams.

Bellevue's twenty doctors could do little to alleviate the situation. They agreed that an adequate hospital was a must for the Eastside.

During the war years of the 1940s, fund raising for a community hospital began. A citizen's committee studied the feasibility and in 1951 three possible sites were considered. The following year a joint report of the State Health Department and the County Planning Commission deplored the lack of such a facility, and this gave rise to formation in 1953 of the Overlake Memorial Hospital Association with a 25-man board of directors. Many kinds of drives to raise funds were conducted—everything from children collecting bottles for salvage to benefit ball games.

The association purchased six tracts of land amounting to seven acres in all. So much confidence was expressed in the projected hospital that private homes were put up as a guarantee for bank loans. The hospital association assumed full responsibility for planning and financing. While it was able only to cover the cost of a building with 50 beds, future expansion was taken into consideration.

The hospital opened in October 1960 with 56 beds and has since grown to 218. It performs more than ordinary community service and is equipped for many specialties. It has a trauma center, 24-hour surgical staff, two Medic I vehicles, and is the third busiest emergency department in King County, with 25,000 persons streaming through it every year. In 1984 its name was changed to Overlake Hospital Medical Center.

By the time the hospital opened, the number of doctors in Bellevue had doubled. The building was expanded several times. Not all of the association's seven acres are devoted to the hospital; a portion was held for physicians' offices and other medical facilities.

Crossroads Mall as it looked when it was finished in 1964. Dick Willard Collection

Crossroads and Lake Hills

Meanwhile growth continued in other directions. Families were moving to the Eastside in increasing numbers, and school attendance was approaching 12,000, quite a change from the days of little wooden buildings. Crossroads Shopping Center appeared on the map in 1961. It and Lake Hills were in unincorporated King County, separated from Bellevue by farms and acreage until annexed in two installments in 1969. While

Lake Hills Library opened in October 1968.

the firm of Bell & Valdez developed many hundreds of acres in that area, much credit for Lake Hills goes to the late R.H. Connor, who died in 1975. He bought approximately 1,200 acres from Modern Homebuilders and got them rezoned into city lots centering on winding Lake Hills Boulevard. Ultimately about 4,000 homes were erected by Connor and several other builders. Ted Valdez was Connor's son-in-law.

When the project started, Crossroads was merely the end of a gravel road terminating at 156th Avenue. The Weyerhaeuser Co. in 1969 formed Quadrant Corp. and promoted the district. In 1955 Lake Hills was advertised as the first major planned community in the Northwest, "a fine residential area in a relaxing country atmosphere." A noteworthy feature was the preservation of a certain number of native trees around the homes. This has been an outstanding characteristic all over Bellevue.

The Evergreen Point Bridge

Though the city was primarily residential, some industries were attracted, including two large grocery distribution centers and an electronics manufacturing company. In 1962 Bellevue Way was widened and paved and the sewage plant was taken over

Phil Shank and Gov. Langlie signing the legislation to appropriate funds for the construction of the Evergreen Point Bridge. Phil Shank Collection

Evergreen Point Floating Bridge, the second bridge to link Bellevue with Seattle, boasts the world's longest floating span. Harriet N. Watters

by Metro. The Evergreen Point Bridge across the lake was ready to open in 1963. For 15 years its location had been the subject of debate. When the day arrived that the first span had paid for itself and the tolls were taken off serious studies began on the feasibility of yet another bridge. After the Evergreen Point Bridge had been completed, bids were called for the first section of Highway 405, the north-south route that links with Interstate 5 but bypasses Seattle. An increasing number of vehicles was overburdening the existing road, Secondary State Highway 2-A, by the time the Second World War ended. Planners had visualized a toll road in its place but this idea was abandoned. When 405 began to take shape it followed much of the proposed toll route. "At the time it ran through open country and there was not much to argue about," said Herman.

The highway work was partially supported by federal funds and the completed project allowed speedy access to Bellevue without the necessity of confronting Seattle traffic.

Civic Growth

For the first time Bellevue acquired a city hall of its own in 1964. It moved out of rented quarters into a new structure on the ground where Clark Sturtevant once had lived. During the following year the municipality took over the buildings and equipment of Fire Department 14, which had been staffed by volunteers who were paid $7 for each call. Fifteen persons were on the new staff. The several firehouses had been established in the late 1940s and early 1950s.

Civic groups were in favor of opening a community college in Bellevue and in 1965 the State Legislature approved the plan. The college moved into temporary quarters in Newport High School, remaining there until a new campus was completed in 1967. By then it had 2,200 students.

School attendance (within the Bellevue school district) continued to increase with the post World War baby boom and in 1970 the number of pupils in the district had doubled and reached 24,000, with the accompanying need for new buildings. In 1977 the peak was reached and 2,200 teachers were employed. Then enrollment began to level off, a few rooms were empty, then several buildings were closed and the pupils were transferred elsewhere by bus. Their place has been taken in some instances by students of private schools which became tenants. These changes have in no way reflected upon the high quality of education in Bellevue.

Among other achievements the new city government created a Parks Department, which in the beginning had only the several acres comprising

Bellevue Community College under construction prior to 1967. Lake Sammamish and the Cascades are in the background. Bellevue Community College

Students enjoying a beautiful spring day at Bellevue Community College. The planetarium rises in the background. Bellevue Community College

Clyde and Chesterfield beaches (the latter a 60 foot road end where SE 25th Street touched the shore) to administer. By 1982 the department controlled more than 1,000 acres and 36 developed parks, with more in the making. The newest is scheduled for Newcastle Beach and another is planned for the former school district property south of Bellevue Square. The department made a determined effort in Bellefield Park on Mercer Slough to bring back the disappearing wild plant and animal life. As a result, beavers and muskrats still live in the slough. Freshwater mussels are to be found and migrating birds on the Pacific flyway stop there. Herons, kingfishers, horned owls, raccoons, weasels, otters and fox have been sighted.

Another of the unusual parks was the Duey farm on Kelsey Creek, where the rural agricultural atmosphere has been preserved. This park also houses the headquarters of the Bellevue Parks and Recreation Department.

The Character of Bellevue Changes

Already in 1966 Nordstrom had moved into a larger store, ground was broken for a 13-story office building, a couple of junior high schools opened and many business structures and apartments were going up all

Meydenbauer Bay when the scene was beginning to change. City of Bellevue

over. Before the end of the decade the Thunderbird Motor Inn and the Holiday Inn were completed and a convention center was established. More dredging had been done in Mercer Slough, and Bellefield Office Park came into existence.

Progress never ceased. Eastgate Plaza was created. An arts commission was established, followed in 1975 by the opening of an art museum. The Bellevue Philharmonic Orchestra already had been organized in 1969. More banks moved in, and more industrial headquarters rose in the vicinity of Northup Way. In 1977 Bellevue had 70 large manufacturing firms. A national survey in 1980 showed the city had the fourth largest "effective buying income" in the United States.

City boundaries had expanded from time to time with the annexation of areas around the rim. When Bellevue was incorporated it reached to Highway 90 on the south, except for Beaux Arts. With Bellevue Way as its southeast border, the line continued out SE 8th Street to just beyond Highway 405. It zigzagged over toward 132nd Avenue, thence north to Northup Way and west to the present boundary of Clyde Hill, which it followed on 89th Avenue south to the lake shore.

Small tracts began to be added at the north end and close to the

Kirkland boundary. Some extended north of Highway 520, including the Pikes Peak neighborhood. By 1957 the city took in Newport Hills and Lake Lanes. These were followed with annexations of Sherwood Forest, Woodridge and Crossroads in 1964; Wilburton, Somerset and the vicinity of Bridle Trails in 1967; Lake Hills and some of the Lake Sammamish shore in 1969 and many other smaller tracts. Altogether more than 60 separate annexations took place in 26 years. Although these included parts of Hilltop and Cougar Mountain, Factoria remained an unincorporated area, almost completely surrounded by Bellevue.

In 1976 the Seattle *Post-Intelligencer* interviewed several Bellevue residents about the way their city had changed in character, "outgrowing its quaint old Main Street." The city's accessibility to two freeways and its pleasant country atmosphere encouraged business and manufacturing firms to locate here. The resulting jobs required a greater work force than Bellevue had to offer, thus causing an increase in rush hour traffic both ways to and from Seattle. By May 1982, 75,000 cars daily were crossing the Evergreen Point Bridge. In that year, over 52 million vehicles crossed the two Lake Washington bridges. Taking them together, the daily volume of traffic increased by 5,000 cars in each of the preceding four years.

About 80 percent of the downtown area was devoted to automobiles, for in time Bellevue became almost completely dependent on them. As a result of the stringent on-site parking regulations requiring four parking spaces for every 1,000 square feet of office space, real estate costs in the downtown area skyrocketed. One real estate man declared, "Bellevue is a planner's paradise, but it's a developer's hell."

By 1981 many electronic and software firms had moved into Bellevue. Emphasis was shifting from garden offices to high-rise, and the city's central skyline was changing. Hotel row was a reality, its night illumination shedding a glow over what had been the edge of a swamp in pioneer times.

When the city in the fall of 1981 decided to rezone its downtown area and permit some skyscrapers to be built, its suburban days were over. A land rush and building boom resulted and Bellevue became the hottest real estate market on the West Coast. Property values were pushed up and plans were announced to build more office space in the next five years than had been constructed in all the preceding quarter century.

Bellevue Square vs. Evergreen East

The shopping Square already had become the first target for change as the outcome of a nearly ten-year battle over a proposed rival center.

Interior of the shopping mall. Elevators carry visitors up to the Bellevue Art Museum's new quarters on the third level. Chris Eden, Bellevue Art Museum

The Chapel of Flowers was the scene of many weddings, memorial services and other commemorative events before it became the Bellevue Art Museum. It was destined to vanish when the shopping mall was increased in size. Mrs. Chester N. Green Collection

For a long time a 400-acre unincorporated island existed between Bellevue and Redmond at what is now known as Overlake Park and Evergreen Highlands. Though Redmond annexed it in 1962, its commercial proximity to Bellevue made it seem part of the latter city. Today the average person bound for the Sears store or the Safeco Insurance Company headquarters is not conscious of having crossed the boundary into another municipality.

In this area Bert McNae, a developer, prepared to build an industrial and shopping park to be known as Evergreen East. When it was about to get under way, with the announced inclusion of another large department store, Kemper Freeman, Sr. led the battle to stifle the project, contending that two major shopping centers on the Eastside could not survive. He made it known that he wanted to greatly increase the size of Bellevue

Square. In the mid-70s it already was becoming inadequate. The big stores wanted more space. Though Freeman had been talking of expansion for years, it was the threat of Evergreen East that gave impetus to doubling the size of the mall. As the initial step, Bellevue Square was sold to a trust in 1966, with the Freeman family and the Elwell Case family forming a corporation, Bellevue Square Managers, to handle the leasing and do the developing.

The Evergreen East controversy had accentuated the public opposition to more removal of trees, spreading of asphalted areas and changing the environment; therefore the Freemans, father and son Kemper Jr., and their associates decided to stay within the original bounds of the Square, building upward instead of out.

The Square Expands

The trust immediately went to work on plans for converting the open Square to a multi-level mall. The needed capital for expansion, the largest loan ever given to a shopping center, was obtained from private sources in Hartford, Conn. The $100 million development opened in May, 1981. When completed it was expected to have 196 stores of all sizes and would be the state's largest shopping center. All three of its general stores— Nordstrom's, Frederick & Nelson and J.C. Penney's—expanded and moved either entirely or partially into new buildings. A fourth department store, the Bon Marche, prepared to open in the summer of 1984.

With its increased size the exterior of the mall was not beautiful. One architectural critic said, "It maintains an incredible fortress-like wall to the outside world."

As expansion continued a generation of buildings disappeared one after the other, among them the Chapel of the Flowers, scene of many marriages and memorial services. After serving as an art museum it suc-

The present look of roof-top parking at the shopping mall, as viewed from the air. The white structure toward the right is the Bon Marche, facing Bellevue Way.
Harriet N. Watters

cumbed to wreckers and the space it occupied is part of the parking fa-cilities adjoining J.C. Penney's. A bank building, formerly housing the Square management offices and a low brick building housing Strom's cleaning establishment for many years were the last to go. All of this hap-pened at an accelerated pace because of the need to provide more park-ing areas. When the construction period ends it will be offset by fresh plantings of trees and planned improvements such as an outdoor arcade or pedestrian corridor along NE 6th Street from the front entrance of the mall with a fountain and greenery.

Because Bellevue takes its landscaping seriously, most of the trees and shrubbery of the old center were dug up and made ready to replace as part of a new landscaping scheme. In addition, 700 new trees were to be planted.

Remembering Freeman's slogan, "Parking invites people to come and do business," construction plans included multi-level parking garages for 3,800 cars. Much as the city wished to avoid it, pay parking came in 1983, not for shoppers but for workers who leave their automobiles all day. Much parking has had to go underground, but shopper's spaces are still free. Increased bus service may relieve the situation for employees.

Kemper Freeman, Sr. lived to see many of his dreams come true. When he died on October 20, 1982 at the age of 72, it was said that probably no other man had done more to mold the shape of the city. His original Square, carved out of an orchard, had only 16 stores; at the time of his death it was being visited by an average of 26,000 shoppers on an average day, and sometimes as many of 50,000. The Square's several thousand employees represent 15 to 20 per cent of all the Bellevue downtown workers.

More evidence of the rising skyline. The building to the lower right is appropriately named Skyline Tower. It faces NE 4th. Harriet N. Watters

Looking west toward the mall and Meydenbauer Bay. The telephone company building is in the center foreground. Harriet N. Watters

Rising Skyline

The city's growth did not stop at the edge of the Square. The skyline which had begun sprouting in the 1970s was changing each month with the erection of tall structures. The Skyline Tower is 24 stories high, One Bellevue Center 22 stories and Plaza Center 16 stories. Another high rise of 24 stories and two more tall ones are in various stages of planning. The one for Pacific Northwest Bell alone was designed to provide space for 1,350 employees.

Such buildings never were visualized by the original city planners. The City Planning Department states that back in 1954 building heights in the city center were limited to 40 feet, which explains why Puget Power had to get permission for its extra floor. From then on there was no occasion for another ruling until 1981 when a 20 floor (or 200 foot) limit went on the books. But builders have the debate going again and are attempting to circumvent City Council attempts to head off any high-rise developments on the fringe of downtown. Although the city has a

Close-up of the East Channel bridge, which at 70 feet is high enough so that pleasure craft can pass under it. Harriet N. Watters

master plan for the central area, the council is being urged to conduct a review of high-rise zoning along the periphery of downtown. Changes would increase problems of traffic congestion, a matter for which planners supposed they had taken adequate steps to control.

Even highways are widening and altering. An additional 405 interchange at NE Fourth Street will be constructed to relieve congestion en route to Bellevue Square. The newest visible addition to travel routes is the high bridge at Enatai over the East Channel, completed in 1981 to replace the second span at this lake crossing. The earlier steel and cement structure no longer was wide enough to accommodate anticipated traffic over widened Highway 90 and, besides that, a high level connection was needed for marine traffic when the old bulging drawspan was removed from the main Lake Washington floating bridge.

In 1940, if Bellevue had a slogan, it was "Across the bridge to gracious living." The desire of Eastsiders was to preserve the country atmosphere and yet have everything a big city could furnish. They seem to have achieved this, but in the course Bellevue has endured growing pains. It is still growing in population, traffic congestion and area; possibly in the future it may annex Factoria and Cougar Mountain.

Art Skolnick, who inventoried King County's historical sites, observed, "Bellevue is probably one of the best examples in a metropolitan area where unrestricted growth has obliterated any evidence of historical beginnings."

It has become a sophisticated, ultra-modern city that for the most part, except in its center, has preserved its affinity with the outdoors and retained the beauty of its trees. It has endeavored to sustain an uncluttered, well-cared-for look. Its policy is to confine all major new office construction to the central business district, which has been rezoned for more intensive development.

Given the city's excellent location, its surrounding scenery and clean atmosphere, it has thus far justified the name bestowed on it by the pioneer settlers—Belle-Vue.

Author's Notes on the 1984 Edition

Much of this book is based on personal interviews with Eastside pioneers I had in the 1950s when I was on the staff of the *Seattle Times Sunday Magazine* and, after, with long-time residents whose recollections I gathered for my column in the *Journal-American*.

Among those to whom I am indebted for their reminiscences are:

Several descendants of Aaron Mercer
Roland G. Burrows
Isaac Bechtel, Jr.
Helen Thode Boddy
Allan Sharpe
Virginia Lang
Mr. and Mrs. Donald A. Wilson
Mrs. William J. Wilkins
Fred Sorenson
Cameron (Kay) Neumann
Mrs. Ella Stennett
Mrs. James Godsey
Mrs. Kathleen Leptich
Dr. Raymond A Kardong
Francis Hammarstrom
Mrs. Helen Ditty
John F. Herman
Sam Boddy
Dick Skinner

Alla Olds Luckenbill
Irene Larsen Clayton and Dolores Schroeder
Cano Numoto
William S. Lagen
Kemper Freeman, Sr.
Hewitt Jackson
Russell Whaley
Paul T. Vander Hoek
Laura Emery Gilmore
Walter Mercer
W.K. Campbell
John Kelfner
Robert A. Hennig
Patricia Sandbo
Mrs. E.L. Van Tyne
Mrs. Sadie Corey
Mr. and Mrs. William Ottinger

and to Nancy Pryor of the Washington State Library for enabling me to borrow film of the Bureau of Land Management tract books for the 1870s.

I received further help from my articles in *The Seattle Times* files, bound copies of *The Reflector* in the Bellevue Library, early files of the *Intelligencer* and the *Seattle Post-Intelligencer*, the *Eastside Journal*, *The American* and the *Journal-American*. Other sources were:

Records at Marymoor Museum
The Bellevue Planning Department
Art Kramer in behalf of Puget Power
The Pacific Northwest Bell public relations department

U.S. Army Corps of Engineers records in the Federal Records
    Center
Scrapbooks in the University of Washington Library
The Bellevue Parks Department
Angie Burt Bowden's book, "Early Schools of Washington Territory"
Elizabeth Wright's book, "Miller Freeman"

I wish to acknowledge the debt of gratitude I owe to Carolyn Farnum and Floyd W. Hancock for verifying from their records many of the facts about land ownership in this book.

ABOUT THE AUTHOR

Lucile McDonald, a descendant of Oregon pioneers, was a journalist both in this country and in distant parts of the world. She wrote a number of juvenile fiction, young adult and adult nonfiction books. For many years she was on the staff of the *Seattle Times Sunday Magazine* and traveled throughout the state gathering materials and researching hundreds of articles, many with a historical slant. Mrs. McDonald made her home on the east side of Lake Washington beginning in 1944 and was known for her column "Eastside Yesterdays" in the *Journal-American*. Among books written in her later years were *The Lake Washington Story*, *Swan Among the Indians*, *Coast Country*, *Where the Washingtonians Lived*, *The Arab Marco Polo*, *Garden Sass* and the award-winning *Windmills, an Old-New Energy Source*.

NOTES TO MCDONALD'S ORIGINAL TEXT

1. A land developer in 1960, while operating a bulldozer in the Somerset community, uncovered shellfish fossils dating from 40 million years ago. They were in sandstone at an elevation of 675 feet above sea level. Among them were clams, geoducks, snails and aturia, related to the nautilus. Presence of this last creature confirmed a theory that much of the Pacific Northwest was once submerged under a tropical ocean.

2. A government survey of 1871 said in wet seasons the level of the lake rose as much as four feet and in dry seasons dropped one and a half feet below normal. An oldtimer asserted that the level might vary seven to ten feet during a year and that once his father's dock was completely under water. It is generally accepted that the variation was six feet. In any case, the high water frequently menaced farm lands in the vicinity of Renton. A scientist who made a study of the lake believed that 1100 years ago it may have been 12 to 20 feet lower than now.

3. John Kinnear arrived in Seattle from Illinois in 1883, several years after his better-known brother, George. John was a member of the territorial legislature, helped frame the state constitution, ran for governor and for some years was in the state senate. He died in 1912.

4. Settlers could expect to encounter wild animals in the Eastside's forest. The county commissioners in 1880 offered bounties of $3 each for scalps of cougar, black or gray wolves and black bear and $1 for wildcats. The offer was revoked a year later.

5. Apparently geological reports show no evidence of coal in this area. It could have been coal dust deposited by Coal Creek.

6. A resident of Medina, Floyd Croft, told of staying in "a little old log house that was lived in by every family who built over here." On the door was the inscription, "A.S. Burrows erected on October 11, 1889."

7. The *City of Latona* was a small craft built on Lake Union. In 1892 she was making two round trips daily to Bellevue, charging 25 cents each way. An amusing story was told about one crossing. A woman passenger was taking a dishpan home and set it on the foredeck. A joker picked it up, climbed on top of the cabin and clapped the pan down over the smokestack. This smothered the fire, stopped the boat, and the smoke chased people out of the cabin. The joker let out a yell that if he didn't get

across by a certain time he was going to lose $150 on a deal. Somebody saw the pan and removed it but the woman was unhappy about its coating of soot.

8. Miller from 1886 through 1888 figured as defendant in a series of murder trials related to the death of James Manning Colman, a Kennydale resident. Finally the charge was dismissed, but Miller's health was ruined. He died in 1893.

9. The log cabin in the park was not Kelsey's. It was moved from NE 7th and 127th Avenue NE, where it was erected in 1888 by Daniel W. Frazer for his relatives, Fanny and Steven Rathbun. It was moved twice, the last time in 1974.

10. John D. Houghton, a logger from Maine, and his wife Annie, arrived in Seattle in 1885 and a few months later bought 80 acres across Bellevue Way from where the North Towne Shopping Center is located. He had to cut down large trees to make room for a house constructed of boards he floated across the lake on a raft and dragged uphill with oxen. After Mr. Houghton died Annie took in orphan children to live with her until she married Irvin J. Blakney.

11. The Buckley homestead's northern boundary was two blocks south of the Apple Valley development and may have inspired its name. Old fruit trees are still visible around there.

12. From a *Journal-American*, July 10, 1978 article by Lucile McDonald.

13. It is related that John Zwiefelhofer, not satisfied with the price farmers were being offered for a railroad right-of-way through their land, went with a shotgun to where the crew and teams were at work and stopped them until men came from Seattle to negotiate a more favorable settlement.

14. In 1894 Peter Saal and his family moved north of Meydenbauer Bay and near the Downeys. Saal later had his own greenhouse and was the first to employ Japanese. He was disliked because of this, and one time when Seattle merchants scorned his flowers on this account, he became angry and dumped the rejected load in Lake Washington. Saal died in 1936 at the age of 78. A.F. Haas, who considered himself one of Bellevue's earliest boosters, spent his last years residing at the Ledges, where he passed away in March, 1926.

15. Hans Nickelson was granted a homestead patent in 1884 in what is now Clyde Hill and sold parts of it to Soren Sorenson and Adolph Peterson, who arrived shortly after Downey. Their farms were near 92nd Avenue NE and the beach at its foot became Peterson's Landing. Sorenson in 1889 owned all the remainder of Nickelson's claim. He had a windmill, raised strawberries, hay, chickens and cows, and sold butter, eggs and produce in the city.

16. A 1912 map of Bellevue had some strange street names such as Wildwood Avenue, Linden Avenue, Cedar, Alder and Ronda Streets. In Moorland there were Zarigda, Grenada and Alhambra Streets. Others were Oriental, Woodland and Illora.

17. The *Leschi* was the first automobile ferry servicing Medina and Bellevue. Launched December 6, 1913, she cost $87,000 and could carry 50 automobiles and teams. Her speed was 15 knots. She was owned and operated by King County and was described as a sidewheeler 156 feet long. She was partially built at a yard on the East Waterway, then disassembled and hauled overland to the foot of Genesee Street near the Taylor mill and reconstructed. The *Leschi* was remodeled in 1930 and given a diesel engine. When the bulky paddle boxes were removed this allowed more space for cars, which previously had to be backed into the areas around them. In the beginning charges were assessed by weight, 75 cents the round trip for light cars, 90 cents for a medium one and $1.20 for a heavy automobile.

18. Norman Blye provides talks to historical groups entitled "Ferry Tales of Lake Washington." In his program he tells the story of the ferry *Dawn* that went to Bellevue through heavy fog to pull the burning whaling vessel away from the dock.

19. Now the Boys and Girls Club property at 100th Avenue.

20. Delbert and his wife in July 1926 bought the lot and residence from G.W. and Florence Crooks and turned it into a popular restaurant and tea room.

21. Ditty said, "I paid $6,250 for ten acres. That was roughly one and a half cents a square foot." He sold them to Kemper and Miller Freeman so cheaply they were embarrassed, his widow said. "Heck," he told the Freemans, "I'd rather have given it to you as long as you improve it."

22. The same year the Bellevue Water District was laying mains, a news item told of the collapse of William Raine's windmill and water tank.

23. Qualheim Road took its name from Carl O. Qualheim, who settled on former Mercer land, platted it, and dealt in real estate.

24. Bill Little operated the feed store five years, but so many persons owed outstanding bills that he decided to close it. Fred Sorenson was the next owner. Kathleen Leptich said, "My father, Joe Kardong, also had a pot belly stove in his place and in winter people would come in and warn their hands over it and stay awhile. People had time to talk in those days."

25. A thief in 1937, upon learning that Bellevue had no town marshal and that a constable came only occasionally and then only in daytime, thought he could take the community to "a cleaning." He was rudely disillusioned and landed in jail.

26. Lacey Murrow was the Director of the Washington State Department of Highways and Chief Engineer of the Washington State Toll Bridge Authority. He was also the brother of Edward R. Murrow, the well known news commentator.

27. Naslund had been associated with a grocery at Wilburton during the First World War and later did concrete construction.

28. Freeman's statement did not accurately describe the banking situation. Although the First Bank of Bellevue had closed some years earlier and its assets were absorbed by the Kirkland bank, leaving the town again without a financial institution, the Washington State Bank was opened in the old quarters on Main Street about 1942. It is interesting to note that the building which was the first home of *The American* was occupied successively by the first Bank of Bellevue, Meta Burrows Pharmacy and the Washington State Bank. After the newspapers vacated the basement the public library took it over in 1957.

29. In 1952 Bruce Helberg and Clarence Laframboise, Auburn publisher, bought *The American*. In 1976 John McClelland, of Longview, combined it with the *Eastside Journal* of Kirkland, moved it into new quarters and it became the daily *Journal-American*.

30. A.A. Nordhoff in 1945 opened an air field on a tract south of Phantom Lake. At its peak in the mid-1970s it was home for 130 planes and was rated the state's ninth busiest airport. Nordhoff operated a flying school beside the 2,325-foot long airstrip. His business was isolated out there in the brush, but gradually the 300 acres shrank. Some of it was sacrificed to construction of Highway 90 across the southern end. The field was finally forced to close in May 1983.

FURTHER READING

Although Bellevue has not been the subject of extensive historical research, there is a greater amount of material concerning the city and specific aspects of it than one might first suspect.

For the most part, we have concentrated on readily available, published items about Bellevue, but the holdings of the Bellevue Historical Society deserve special notice. The Society holds a considerable amount of writings and files about the city, its people, and its history. The Society is engaged in an Oral History Project, and it is participating in the Eastside Japanese-American History Project in conjunction with the Japanese American Citizens League.

There is an abundant amount of writing by Lucile McDonald. Although her own autobiography, *A Foot in the Door*, closes before her Bellevue years, that volume is an interesting account of her life, augmented by Lorraine McConaghy's short introduction. McDonald's history of Bellevue, republished here, and her history of Lake Washington draw together much of the story of the Eastside. Her many newspaper articles add more; McConaghy has collected 101 of them in *Lucile McDonald's Eastside Notebook* for which the editor has also written a short biography.

A capsule description of Bellevue appears in Clarence B. Bagley's *History of King County[,] Washington*, published in 1929. An early history of Bellevue for which much information was assembled is *The Bellevue Story* by a local teacher, Connie Jo Squires. In 1989, Squires published a small, shorter edition for and illustrated by children. *Columbia Magazine,* Summer 1997, includes Charles P. LeWarne's somewhat nostalgic article about the four stages his home town has passed through. *Bellevue and the New Eastside* by Bob Welch is a big, colorful book that stresses businesses. Robert Karolevitz's family-commissioned biography of Kemper Freeman,

Sr., also includes a running account of Bellevue's history, much of it placing the subject's life and work in its local context.

Several publications by governmental and public organizations are extremely useful for understanding Bellevue. The City published a valuable study of historic spots in *Bellevue Historic and Cultural Resources Survey* by Caroline Tobin and Lee Pendergrass in 1993 and an updated version in 1997. Extremely useful for understanding recent and present-day Bellevue is *Bellevue Environmental Scan* which the City published in 1999 along with a short "overview" version. Also helpful is the fund of information in the Bellevue School District's *Profiles* for 1997–1998. The Eastside Leadership Committee sponsored Richard Larsen's *Eastside Story* in which community leaders express views on the area's major concerns.

There are several accounts of Bellevue neighborhoods or nearby communities. Lorraine McConaghy's Ph.D. dissertation on Lake Hills is thorough and interpretive and includes much about the larger Bellevue as well. Victor Scheffer has written a fine, detailed account of Hilltop, the cooperative community of which he was a founder and 45-year resident. Junius Rochester's story of Lakelure, a Medina mansion, also tells about its illustrious residents and that community. Reminiscences by long-time citizens contributed to Jeanne Whitney's account of Yarrow Point.

A number of organizations have printed their histories in various form. The Bellevue Historical Society has copies of many. Notable is Hugh Martin's history of the First Congregational Church which is augmented by a later account by Don and Kathleen Williams. Historical material about other churches is in a church history file at the Society. The Meydenbauer Yacht Club has also published its history. A year-by-year account of the Overlake Service League from 1911 to 1959 gives a good view of their activities.

In addition to the Kemper Freeman biography, a few others are of interest. Bert McNae, who was involved in the days of heady development, has written an autobiography. Judge William J. Wilkins was a long-time Bellevue resident who tells much of his personal life and the houses which he and his wife built, renovated, moved, and lived in. James Wallace and Jim Erickson's *Hard Drive* tells a bit about Microsoft's Bellevue era.

As Bellevue began to attract regional attention during its suburban years, newspaper and magazine accounts became more frequent, and their tones ranged from high praise to ridicule. One of the more interesting is Rillmond Schear's account in *Seattle Magazine* for June 1965. Several useful books on American suburbs include Robert Fishman's *Bourgeois Utopias* and Kenneth Jackson's *Crabgrass Frontier. Edge City* by Joel Garreau provided insight and a framework for interpreting modern-day Bellevue.

Marymoor Museum has the Rody Burrows Collection available for research. Also available are parts of the Whaley and Lagen collections.

Bagley, Clarence B. *History of King County [,] Washington.* 2 vols. Chicago, Seattle: The S. J. Clarke Publishing Company, 1929, I:861–2.

Bellevue Environmental Scan. Bellevue, WA: City of Bellevue, 1999.

Bellevue Environmental Scan: An Overview. Bellevue, WA: City of Bellevue, 1999.

Dupar, Robert W., and Roger R. Huffman. *Meydenbauer Yacht Club: History of the Bay and the Club.* 1987.

Fishman, Robert. *Bourgeois Utopias: The Rise and Fall of Suburbia.* New York: Basic Books, Inc., 1987.

Garreau, Joel. *Edge City: Life on the New Frontier.* New York, London, Toronto, Sydney, Auckland: Doubleday, 1991.

Jackson, Kenneth. *Crabgrass Frontier: The Suburbanization of the United States.* New York, Oxford: Oxford University Press, 1985; paperback edition, 1987.

Karolevitz, Robert F. *Kemper Freeman, Sr. and the Bellevue Story.* Mission Hill, SD: The Homestead Publishers, 1984.

Larsen, Richard W. *Eastside Story.* n. p.: [Eastside Leadership Committee], *ca.* 1997.

LeWarne, Charles P., "Bellevues I Have Known: Reflections on the Evolution of an 'Edge City'," *Columbia: The Magazine of Northwest History*, 11:3–9 (Summer 1997).

Martin, Hugh W. *A History of the First Congregational Church of Bellevue, Washington: A Continuing Story*.

McConaghy, Lorraine, ed. *Lucile McDonald's Eastside Notebook: 101 Local History Vignettes*. Redmond, WA: Marymoor Museum, 1993.

McConaghy, Lorraine. *No Ordinary Place: Three Postwar Suburbs and Their Critics*. Ph.D. dissertation, University of Washington, 1993.

McDonald, Lucile. *Bellevue: Its First 100 Years*. Fairfield, WA: Ye Galleon Press, 1984.

McDonald, Lucile. *A Foot in the Door: The Reminiscences of Lucile McDonald*. With Richard McDonald. Foreword by Lorraine McConaghy. Pullman, WA: Washington State University Press, 1995.

McDonald, Lucile. *The Lake Washington Story: A Pictorial History*. Seattle: Superior Publishing Company, 1979.

McNae, Bert. *Vision Guts & Money: The Bert McNae Story*. With Nancy Way. Redmond, WA, 1995.

History of Overlake Service League, 1911–1959. In Bellevue Historical Society.

Rochester, Junius. *Lakelure: A Tale of Medina, Washington*. Seattle: Tommi Press, 1993.

Schear, Rillmond, "The Great Big Boom in Bellevue," *Seattle Magazine*, 2:28–37, 45–47 (June 1965).

Scheffer, Victor B. *Hilltop: A Collaborative Community*. Bellevue: Bellevue Historical Society, 1994.

Squires, Connie Jo. *The Bellevue Story*. Bellevue, 1967; children's edition, 1989.

Tobin, Caroline C., and Lee F. Pendergrass. *Bellevue Historic and Cultural Resources Survey*. Bellevue: City of Bellevue Design and Development Department, 1993; updated version, 1997.

Wallace, James, and Jim Erickson. *Hard Drive: Bill Gates and the Making of the Microsoft Empire*. New York, Chicester, Brisbane, Toronto, Singapore: John Wiley & Sons, Inc., 1992.

Welch, Bob. *Bellevue and the New Eastside: A Contemporary Portrait*. n. p.: Windsor Publications, Inc., 1989.

Whitney, Jeanne L. *Yarrow: a place: an historical commentary on lives and times during early development of Yarrow Point.* Yarrow Point, WA, 1976.

Wilkins, William J. *The Sword and the Gavel, by The Last of the Nuremberg Judges William J. Wilkins: An Autobiography.* With Eleanor Elford Cameron. Seattle: The Writing Works, A Division of Morse Press, 1981.

Williams, Don and Kathleen. *The Little White Church That Grew: A History of the Bellevue First Congregational Church, U. C. C., 1896–1996.* 1996.

INDEX